just give me
a little piece
of quiet

just give me a little piece of quiet

60 mini-retreats for a mom's soul

Lorilee Craker

Grand Rapids, Michigan

Published by Fleming H. Revell
a division of Baker Publishing Group
P.O. Box 6287, Grand Rapids, MI 49516-6287

MOPS edition published 2005
ISBN 0-8007-3120-4

Printed in the United States of America

Library of Congress Cataloging-in-Publication Data

Craker, Lorilee.
Just give me a little piece of quiet : 60 mini-retreats for a mom's soul / Lorilee Craker.
p. cm.
Includes bibliographical references.
ISBN 0-8007-5996-6 (pbk.)
1. Mothers—Prayer-books and devotions—English. I. Title
BV4847.C75 2005
242'.6431—dc22 2004026794

Published in association with the literary agency of Alive Communications, Inc., 7680 Goddard Street, Suite 200, Colorado Springs, CO 80920.

To George and Pat Vanderlaan,
for taking us under your wings and
enfolding us so generously into your family.
We love you.

contents

acknowledgments

My abiding thanks to the following people for support, encouragement, fine-tuning, stories, and friendship:

Friends: Bonnie Anderson, Carla Klassen, Nancy Rubin, Stephanie Nelson, Lisa Freire, Becky Wertz Walker, Rachel Arnold, Mary Jo Haab, and Sheri Rodriguez.

Friend/Writers: Laura Jensen Walker, Lisa Bergren, Julie Barnhill, Tracy Groot, Jen Abbas, Julie Johnson, and Beth Lagerborg.

Relatives: Abe and Linda Reimer, Ken and Linda Craker, Dan and Tina Reimer, Mike and Jodi Connell, and Lorraine and Tracy Bush.

Baker Book House types: Dwight Baker, Mary Wenger, and Paula Gibson. Special thanks to the following: To Twila Bennett, for a decade of friendship, your savvy marketing mind, and lots of enthusiasm! To Jennifer Leep, for your "light" editing, your graceful style, and for being excited about this little book.

To Ann Byle, without whose constant encouragement and bizarre sense of humor I would surely be bereft.

And especially to Doyle, who carried so much of the parenting and household stuff while I was writing this book, and my sons, Jonah and Ezra, who must have thought their mother lived in the basement there for a while! I love all three of you.

introduction

Recently I was at an airport gate with my two sons, having heard the disturbing news that our flight would be delayed by an hour or more. My heart sank. Flying with toddlers is just plain stressful, and my particular tot—with his will of iron ore and his strong dislike of sitting still—was at that juncture jumping on my last nerve. All the clever little plane toys I had packed had been checked already, and all I wanted to do was get on the plane—our last leg of a long day's journey—and fly home.

You know how, as moms, we kind of "budget" our energy and patience for whatever time frame we're dealing with? I had calculated about two hours more of travel time until I could hand my darling cherubs over to their doting dad, who would be waiting at the appointed time at the airport in Grand Rapids. My stamina budget was set at two hours, not three or four, and I was sure my estimated energy expenditures would dry up long before the blessed sight of Gerald R. Ford International Airport.

"Can you believe this?" A cute blond mom of two rolled her eyes as we shared our misery. "Yeah, this is real nice," I agreed, my maternal instincts taut against the possibility that my turbo tot could—and would—dart out at any second, possibly right in front of one of those scary airport golf carts zooming around the terminal.

Without really discussing it, we two waylaid traveling clans hunkered down and waited out the delay together. Snacks were procured or dug out of bags, and the six of us sat cross-legged on the airport floor having a picnic of sorts. The mom and I chatted about our kids—her girl and my oldest were the same age, and her boy and my little guy were close; the perils of flying with kids; weight loss; preschool; favorite movies; and everything else under the sun. (I must admit, when her travel-weary three-year-old started choking his big sister, my tension started to unravel. Isn't that an awful thing to admit? Somehow, watching other kids behave badly was almost refreshing after untangling my own children's snarls all day long.) Evidently even put-together moms like my new acquaintance, Mrs. California, had times when their children were out of control—in public!

Then this wonderful woman suddenly produced a portable DVD player from her bag and popped in a *Dora the Explorer* video. The two little boys lay down on their tummies, heads in hands, and watched the cartoon. My older son, Jonah, taught his new West Coast pal—a very pretty six-year-old, whom he didn't even mind losing to—how to play Go Fish. Savvy Mommy and I were actually free to have some girl talk. And so it was that my little family passed a very enjoyable hour in the airport terminal. When the gate attendant announced that the bird that had flown into the airplane's engines had been extracted and the plane was cleared to board, I was almost disappointed we didn't have more time together.

What does this little episode have to do with the book you hold in your hands? It illustrates the vital need for moms to connect with each other, to have down time to relax a bit and "re-create" themselves. I definitely was re-created by the gift of that experience. I have no doubt God sent that mom to me—and me to her—at a critical moment when we were about to lose it.

God is full of gifts for us moms. One of those gifts is time—when we take it—to revive the spiritual, gifted, beautiful woman inside that meat-cutting, fight-refereeing, sleep-deprived chick our kids refer to as "Hey, Mom." With each "mini-retreat," you will be able to step off the mommy treadmill for a little while, get outside your wipe-a-nose workday, and gain perspective, encouragement, and rejuvenation. You'll find readings here about adoption, mommy body image, baby names, friendship with other moms—even sex! (Now, if you've forgotten what that is, perhaps it'll come back to you!)

Some of these readings are serious and reflective, but hopefully many of them will get you to crack a grin. Maybe you'll even experience the kind of "been-there-glad-I'm-not-there-right-now" kind of refreshment I got from the whole choking incident! Yes, in me and my mommy-in-the-trenches stories, you will discover a real mother, warts and all, who loves her kids like crazy but also makes mistakes. I wish and pray that you will come away from this book with a sense of connection to another mom and to the part of you possibly buried under the good work of mothering. Most of all, though, I hope you are pointed, over and over again, to the one who loves you lavishly, pours out his wisdom and grace to cover every situation, and wants so much to give you a little piece of quiet.

1: i'm not the maid

In repentance and rest is your salvation, in quietness and trust is your strength.

Isaiah 30:15

Do you ever feel that way too much of day-to-day motherhood is housework (or just plain work)? Sometimes it seems that all I do is cook meals for the kids, do their laundry (a world without end, amen!), put away their clothes, pick up their toys, and organize their stuff. Housework is simply not my gift. I often look around my cluttered yet cozy abode, with its piles of magazines, scattered toys, and stray socks, and wonder where Alice from *The Brady Bunch* is when I need her. The physical work that goes into mothering is considerable. Even just basic care and feeding of a child can consume a surprising amount of time and stamina.

Much harder, though, than the daily domestic grind of household chores is the emotional work that goes into parenting. I'm talking about listening to a child prattle on endlessly, trying to give her your full attention but struggling to concentrate on what she's saying, breaking up skirmish after skirmish in the never-ending sibling rivalries that exist in every home, and willing yourself to be patient with a little one who is jumping on your last nerve.

Whether physical or emotional, too much work can leave you depleted of both the physical stamina you need to chase a toddler and the mental verve required to comfort a colicky baby who's been screaming for three hours. Often, motherhood taps into both types of energy.

Somehow though, as moms, we live by an unspoken code that dictates that we give and give until there's no more left to give. We often put impossible expectations on ourselves that are, in the end, toxic to our sanity, our marriages, and ultimately our families.

I remember David Letterman riffing on his mom's penchant for telling her kids, "I do and do and *do* for you guys." If you believe that being a "good" mother means you have to, like Mom Letterman, do and do and *do* until you've consumed every smidgen of energy and personal passion, no wonder you're too tired for the fun elements of life with kids. "Maternal perfectionism and excessive self-sacrifice is a treadmill with no off switch," says author and therapist Valerie Davis-Raskin. How can we turn that treadmill off today?

Only you can decide that *you* matter, that a little R & R for mom is really a good thing for everyone you love. Lindsey O'Connor is right on with her book title *If Mama Goes South, We're All Going with Her*. If you go south, you can be sure the whole clan is not far behind. So don't go south! Make self-care a priority.

My friend Becky was having a rare "day off," treated by her husband to a full-body Swedish massage and a spa lunch by the pool. As she drifted in and out of consciousness on the massage table, the cares and stresses of the week melting away under her masseuse's touch, Becky was in bliss. Her masseuse, a fellow mom named Loretta, commended Becky on allowing herself to be pampered. "It's really great for moms to take some time for themselves from time to time," Loretta said. "They always go away from here able to give more to their families." The talented and sensible Loretta was absolutely right. Becky went back to her six-month-old baby and her ten-year-old daughter with arms wide open, refueled and regenerated.

Think an afternoon at the spa is selfish? Some of you think half an hour away from the munchkins is selfish, but you're wrong! Mom work is rewarding but also hard. We need to take time for ourselves so we can do our best work with our kids.

Consider how Jesus took time from his critically important mission on earth for solitude and rest: Jesus "got up, left the house and went off to a solitary place," says Mark 1:35. And Matthew 14:23 echoes this idea: "After he had dismissed the crowds, he went up on a mountainside *by himself* to pray. When evening came, he was there alone" (RSV).

We have been given our children as precious gifts from God. We need to rest, relax, and restore ourselves on a regular basis to be the strongest moms we can be.

Anyone who enters God's rest also rests from his own work, just as God did from his.

Hebrews 4:10

2: don't *ever* let me catch you smoking

God, who has called you into fellowship with his Son Jesus Christ our Lord, is faithful.

1 Corinthians 1:9

My friends have been lifesavers time and time again. Lori was my first dear friend. She is the one who secretly taught me to tie my hat when a rather cranky kindergarten teacher was holding me after school. We walked home from school that day hand in hand, new best buddies. Carla, with her zany, irreverent sense of humor and boldness, filled me with a sense of exhilaration that made me forget all about the pain of being shunned by a certain group of eighth-graders. Mary Jo, a fellow young mother, probably prayed me right up and out of a season of intense temptation and spiritual attack. So often when I've needed a hand held, a little tea and sympathy, or a timely bit of insight to gain clarity, my friends have surrounded me with support and strength. Girlfriends, says singer-songwriter Carolyn Arends, are "conduits of grace."

Let me share with you a real and nitty-gritty story about the things we do sometimes for our friends. It comes from Tracy Groot, a novelist and friend of mine who is one of the most honest and authentic people I know. I'll let Tracy tell you her story in her own words:

> My best friend's mother was killed in a car accident. Two years later, I get a call that her father was in a car accident, was in emergency surgery, and might not make it. I flew to the hospital.
>
> I was rushing through the emergency entrance, when I saw Tami and her sister sitting on the curb. I came over, and Tami looked up with red-rimmed eyes, and guilt—she was smoking a cigarette, a habit she'd kicked a few years earlier.
>
> I stood there, looking down at my dearest friend, who at the age of 25 had lost her mother, and at the age of 27, stood an even chance to lose her father in the exact same way. She looked at me with misery and fear on her face, and of all things, guilt that she was smoking a cigarette. What did she think I was going to do? Say, "Tami, look—I know your Dad is in there dying, but buck up. Put out that nasty thing and be brave, little buckaroo." I saw her face, and the guilt broke my heart even more than her fear. I sat down next to her, looked over at her sister who had the pack of cigarettes, and said, "Hey, gimme one of those things."
>
> Kim was shocked. She exchanged glances with Tami, but gave me a cigarette. I didn't know how to smoke. So I asked them to give me smoking lessons. Within moments, I was an expert, bouncing the cigarette between my lips like a hardcore, trying out different cool ways to hold my ciggie, striking poses. Once I actually inhaled, and had a coughing fit to bring up a lung. We laughed our heads off. We were laughing so hard, I almost rolled off the curb. At some point, our laughter subsided, and we smoked in silence. Later, Kim's husband came out to tell us their Dad would make it.
>
> Tami never forgot it. Smoking, that day, turned out to be one of the better things I'd done in my life. (Fortunately, it didn't start a habit. I don't crave cigarettes, but I am overly fond of food. I tell Tami there's not much difference.)

I grew up in a home and church where smoking was akin to axe-murdering, practically, so I can appreciate how far Tracy went out on a limb to come alongside her suffering friend. Tracy's story reminded me that God is the truest friend we could ever have. He always does the right thing to comfort us, to boost our spirits, and to gently nudge us back on the right path. There is no friend who is as invested in our lives, our well-being, and our very souls. Lord, let me reciprocate in some small measure the awesome, glorious friendship you give me!

There is a friend who sticks closer than a brother.
Proverbs 18:24

3: i'll leave the light on for you

As the Father loved Me, I also have loved you;
abide in My love.

John 15:9 NKJV

"Home is where the heart is," the pillow said, cross-stitched with love. In fact, millions of pillows echo that same sentiment, as do lithographic prints, plaques, mugs, and paperweights. "Home Sweet Home" is another favorite of pillow stuffers, while "Welcome Home" is a preferred doormat adage.

Home to me means much more than just the four walls and the roof I'm under now. It's the house on Kingsford Avenue where my parents brought me home from the hospital. The house they sold five years ago. It's the place I still can't drive by without a lump in my throat and a sense of indignation that there are strange cars in the driveway. Home is also the old farmhouse on the Manitoba prairie where my grandparents lived, surrounded by golden wheat and flax and lemon yellow canola. My college neighborhood in downtown Chicago, with its throb of life and humanity, feels like home too.

And home is my house in Alger Heights, where I sometimes still notice with pleasure the paint colors I chose inside and out, the denim slipcovers, and the crisp white shower curtain in the bathroom. We are culture gone crazy for the idea of transforming spaces, extreme makeovers for houses, and decorating savvy. But beyond a splash of paint, a slipcover, and new crown molding is the heartbeat of the home. Whether you live in a mansion or a fixer-upper, the spaces in a home are where you flesh out who you are and how you define the term *life.*

The notion of home is deeply spiritual, too. John 15 talks about what it means to "abide" in God's love, to dwell, to stay, to inhabit. *Abide* and *abode* have the same linguistic roots. The abode in our hearts, where we invite God to live, is a place where we should meet him often and enjoy his company. When we do spend time there, "hanging out" in a place of love and forgiveness, "we come away feeling so nourished, so cherished, so liked that we would rush back to Him whenever we could," says Bruce Wilkinson, author of *Secrets of the Vine* and *The Prayer of Jabez.*[1]

I like the sound of that. When I neglect that abode, I am prey to feeling the opposite: hungry, discontent, fractious, and even abandoned. But how do we, as scattered and distracted mothers of young kids, find our way to the home in our hearts? It has to be intentional, a working into our busy lives the time to cultivate the discipline of abiding. Lisa Tawn Bergren, in her book *God Encounter: Experiencing the Power of Creative Prayer*, harnesses the power of imagination to lead readers to places where they can encounter God in new ways. A cabin deep in a cool, dense forest, a foggy California bay, and a prairie field are a few of the abiding places Lisa takes us to. In one particularly potent prayer experience, readers journey to a rustic beach house to seek God's presence and companionship:

> I've been called away from my chaotic life, from days filled with appointments and schedules and phone meetings. Of demands

> and chores and desires. To this. This quiet, simple old house. Along the edges of the deep. My eyes follow down the highway to the glass wall that fronts the living room. The ocean, from this vantage point, looks slightly convex; I can see the curvature of the earth's surface. I'm a tiny speck on this great big planet. What am I to the Creator? Why do you want me to know you, Jesus? Why do you yearn for my company as much as I yearn for yours? I'm nothing, so insignificant! In this huge wide world, I'm infinitesimal.[2]

Lisa imagines interacting with Jesus in that beach house, pouring out her fears and concerns, listening to his response:

"He comes ever closer and places a light hand on my chest, above my heart. 'If I live here, you'll never miss me again. And if you listen to your heart, you will hear me.'"[3] We can be with God, abiding in his presence, no matter what is whirling around us. And when we make time for it, we can sit in the quiet with him, talking, listening, being reassured of his love and peace. He'll leave the light on for us.

As the deer pants for the water brooks,
so pants my soul for You, O God.

Psalm 42:1 NKJV

4: play fair

Seek justice, encourage the oppressed.
Defend the cause of the fatherless,
plead the case of the widow.
Isaiah 1:17

Kids are justice fiends. "His pizza/cake/Happy Meal toy is bigger/better than mine. No fair!" On and on it goes. This notorious quality of any given child, to seek fairness to the bitter end is actually not a child's worst vice. In fact, I believe we as moms can tap into their zealous quest for fair play and turn it inside out for the good. Instead of indulging every normal kid's fierce self-centeredness, we can intentionally point out ways other people have been gypped and then fulfill our biblical mandate to seek justice.

There's a biblical mandate to seek justice? Yes! I'm glad you asked. References to justice, being impartial, and working to balance the scales on behalf of the poor, the orphaned, the widowed, and the disenfranchised are peppered throughout Scripture.

Take Amos, a shepherd and fig grower who railed against the corrupt, fat-cat lifestyles of many residents of Judah and Israel. Their prosperity as nations had led to corruption in the judicial courts, oppression of the poor, and spiritual smugness. "Hate evil, love good," he ranted, and thankfully his rants were heeded. Israel did turn their hearts back toward their just God.

What does that have to do with you and me and our kids in the twenty-first century? After all, few of us would be guilty of withholding fair trials or actively oppressing the poor. But we are still required to do what we can to help those who can't help themselves. Ignoring injustice and not caring if people are taken care of also constitutes a spiritual problem. "Seek justice, encourage the oppressed," Isaiah 1:17 says. "Defend the cause of the fatherless, plead the case of the widow." How can we as mothers with young children do our part to encourage the oppressed? What kinds of things can we involve our kids in so we can instill a passion for justice? Listen to these examples of "defending the fatherless" and "pleading the case of the widow":

Dave and Kim often hosted a pair of Sudanese teenagers in their home for dinner. Refugees, Enoch and Sonny were among the thousands of "lost boys" who were orphaned by the slaughter of Christians in Sudan. As Dave and Kim's friendship with the boys increased, their own children became aware that not everyone in the world is allowed to worship freely.

Heather organizes a garage sale each year to benefit orphans and widows in the poverty-ravaged land of Haiti. Her kids sell their toys and clothes, knowing that they won't be buying Happy Meals with the proceeds but rather food for hungry children their own age.

Sheri, whose husband is Puerto Rican, is fairly fluent in Spanish. So are her sons, ages seven and five. In the summertime, instead of going to the wading pool or park every day, Sheri brings her boys to a refugee center in town where they befriend Saharawi African refugees who speak Spanish. Through play and the meals they share, the boys are even teaching their new friends some English.

Norm, Todd, and Joel run a car ministry that recently celebrated giving away seventy-five cars. Not everyone is able to donate a car, obviously, but some families have given the automobiles they were about to replace to this ministry. Instead of pocketing a thousand dollars, or whatever the worth of their car, the givers have the satisfaction of knowing that another family is able to secure employment, improve their financial situation, go to doctor's appointments, and experience the many other blessings that transportation brings, blessings you and I probably take for granted.

Our family has been richly rewarded through our friendship with "Grandma Marge," a seventy-six-year-old widow who was recently left even more helpless when her daughter died suddenly. We drive Marge to church, to her small group, and to doctor's appointments, the pharmacy, etc. Sometimes the kids are bored waiting for Marge to get tested or get blood drawn, but I want them to sacrifice in their own way for the good of someone else. I also want them to receive the blessing that comes from practicing the "pure religion" of "visiting widows and orphans in their distress" (James 1:27).

As you can see, working for fairness and justice takes some thought and elbow grease. Your kids may roll their eyes or complain about being out of their comfort zone, but they may also grasp the concept of justice in a way you never dreamed they could.

Let justice roll on like a river,
righteousness like a never-failing stream!

Amos 5:24

5: respect your elders

God sets the lonely in families.

Psalm 68:6

My mom was a thousand miles away; Mrs. Vanderlaan's daughter was around the world in Germany. God knew we needed each other. In the family of faith, we talk about our fellow Christians as sisters and brothers and even as spiritual mothers and fathers. But it wasn't until I was blessed with a Grand Rapids mom and dad and my children were gifted with local grandparents that I understood how very true the bonds of kinship can be with nonrelatives.

Before we had kids, Doyle and I knew George and Pat Vanderlaan because I was a close buddy with their daughter, Rachel. I remembered Mrs. Vanderlaan's visits to our dorm floor at Moody Bible Institute with the best brownies on earth. Our whole floor couldn't wait for Rachel's mom to visit because her baked goods were out of this world.

I had no idea then that this jovial domestic queen would one day become a precious mother figure to me. When Doyle and I moved to Grand Rapids, Rachel and I soon moved from casual friends to something deeper. Her parents, bubbly Pat and salt-of-the-earth George, invited us over for dinner several times, and we very much enjoyed both the laughter at the table and the bounty spread before us. If ever a person was blessed with kitchen skills, it's Mrs. Vanderlaan.

Then Rachel went on the mission field to serve as a dorm parent at a missionary boarding school in the Black Forest. My mom was far away in Canada, and besides that, was at the time in the depths of a six-year clinical depression. Mrs. Vanderlaan's friendliness and keen sense of humor were like a tonic.

When I was in a car accident soon after Rachel left, Mrs. Vanderlaan dropped everything on her own agenda to take care of me for weeks. We would watch decorating shows on the cable channels and talk for hours about anything and everything.

My grandma died less than a week after the accident. Instead of delivering a heartfelt tribute to Grandma at her funeral, I lay at home flat on my back with a broken pelvis. Mrs. Vanderlaan watched me make a scrapbook page dedicated to my grandma and listened to me reminisce with tears and joy. The highlight of those weeks, though, was being served a pan of scrumptious brownies in bed. Yes, you heard right: a *pan* of chocolate decadence in *bed*. It was the height of pampering. Well, after that, Mrs. Vanderlaan had my eternal loyalty, as you can imagine. She was stuck with me!

Our son Jonah was born that same year, and Grandma Pat and Grandpa George were among the first family members we called. They relished their new roles as Jonah's special Grand Rapids grandparents, and we gratefully accepted their dotage. Umpteen dinners have further cemented our family bond—and accentuated our waistlines!—as have countless hours when the Vanderlaans have babysat our kids. Special times have included Fourth of July sleepovers capped off with a flag-waving ride in Grandpa's vintage Chevy in the neighborhood parade and Grandparents' Day at the same Christian school Grandpa George attended half a century ago. Christmases, Mother's Days,

Father's Days, and birthday parties are all memory-making occasions when we've built traditions in our special relationship with the Vanderlaans. The boys loved Grandma's jokes and hugs and the hours spent with Grandpa playing cars on the floor or T-ball in the yard.

And last summer, when Rachel got married, it was only fitting that all four of us Crakers participated, the little boys as handsome ring bearers, Doyle as an usher, and me as a "mature" bridesmaid. It felt for all the world like a family wedding. Maybe because it really was one.

Recently it finally occurred to Jonah that Grandma Pat and Grandpa George were an extra set of grandparents and that neither Doyle nor I were actually raised by them. "She's not really my grandma," Jonah mused about Mrs. V. "She's just a really nice lady who loves me a lot." Oddly, I wasn't really prepared for him to have this revelation. I was slightly saddened that he ever had to come to that conclusion. But Jonah was past six, and he had simply connected the dots.

"Jonah," I began, carefully, knowing this was one of those big moments, "Grandma Pat and Grandpa George love you just as much as Oma and Opa or Grandma and Grandpa Craker. They don't have any grandchildren, and you don't have any grandparents nearby, so they kind of adopted you in a special way."

"Oh, okay," he shrugged. And that was that. I'm sure our other two children, Ezra and Phoebe, will have the same aha! moment that Jonah did. When they do, I'll answer them the same way and marvel again at God's wonderful provision of a bonus family in our lives.

From the fullness of [God's] grace we have all received one blessing after another.

John 1:16

6: 10 9 8 7 6 5 4 3 2 1!

In your anger do not sin. Do not let the sun go down while you are still angry.

Ephesians 4:26

I could have throttled the kid—my kid, as it happens. We were in Winnipeg for my annual week home in the summer, and my five-year-old son had just committed a major social faux pas by wetting his pants in the front lobby of my parents' apartment building. Did I mention he was five? Jonah had been potty trained for a good two-plus years, and for no reason other than he "forgot," my child created a puddle right before the watching—and glaring—eyes of the building manager. Other residents were also giving me the hairy eyeball. I could have shriveled up and died.

Furious, I grabbed his arm and, in as socially acceptable a way as I could muster, dragged him across the lobby to the elevator. I let him have it with a tirade of "You should have known better! How could you? I asked you if you had to go before we left!" Truly, "Mount Momma," as writer Julie Barnhill coined the phrase, had erupted. But that little volcanic blast was nada compared to the flow of lava that spewed the next day when he did it again. Not in front of strangers this time, though. Oh *nooooo*. This incident occurred right before the narrowed eyes of a scary collection of my parents' friends, one who was wound so tight her hair resembled an SOS pad. Let's call her "Lilith."

Yes, my son, who hadn't had an accident for two years, had his second in as many days because he "forgot" again. I was humiliated, mortified, utterly abashed. Clearly I was a terrible mother who couldn't even potty train a five-year-old! Did I mention that scrubby-haired Lilith was childless? Yes, and it was obvious she thought we both were idiots. This "grin-and-bear-it" gathering, which I attended out of reluctant daughterly duty, had quickly disintegrated into a red-faced disaster. As soon as I got Jonah alone, I burst into tears. I cried because I was so confused, shocked, and embarrassed. I cried because I was so angry I couldn't see straight. Once was bad enough, but twice, and in front of *Lilith*?

Why do our kids push our buttons the way they do? Like every other mom who has lost her cool, I later felt as regretful and miserable as I had been irritated and angry. Guilt, every mother's snide constant companion, was compounding my feelings of uselessness. I wish I had been able to take Jonah's accidents in stride, serenely mopping up the two puddles of urine and then later calmly meting out appropriate discipline. But no, I had blown up both times, a little the first time and a lot the second.

Julie Barnhill wrote the book *She's Gonna Blow!* to help other moms like her who struggle with anger toward their kids. She was flooded by letters and emails from readers who had run the yell/cry/feel guilty circuit a few too many times. She reassures all of us who lose it with our beloved children that we are not alone. Even the most longsuffering madre among us has experienced some measure of wrath toward their little ones.

It helps to talk about it with your mom pals, who can look you in the eye with the healing balm of friendship and say, "I've been there too." Choose carefully, though, because you don't want to look in a "Lilith's" eyes and see judgment. Even more important, God is always with you, and his look is tender, full of grace and forgiveness. "The Father of all knows you, and He has seen your struggle and tears," writes Barnhill. "You have never been beyond his reach, though you may believe you are unworthy of such mercy."

"The LORD is compassionate and gracious, slow to anger and abounding in lovingkindness," King David wrote in Psalm 103 (NASB). "For as high as the heavens are above the earth, so great is his lovingkindness toward those who fear Him." When you blow up in anger with your kids, tell them you're sorry and that you love them. Acknowledge Mount Momma, and deal with your anger. Go to God and ask for his forgiveness, mercy, and compassion. Ask him to build self-control, kindness, and gentleness into your spirit. You and I can change, because God can change us!

As far as the east is from the west,
so far has he removed our transgressions from us.
Psalm 103:12

7: what in the world do you think you're doing?

The spirit is willing, but the body is weak.

Matthew 26:41

Kids do the darnedest things, don't they? Really wacky things that make no sense to anyone but them. Case in point: When my teenage babysitter Helen was five, she got a pet goldfish. Though the fish was in a baggie of water when she brought him home, soon he found himself swimming in a glass of milk. Little Helen, heeding her parents' constant refrain to drink milk because it was good for her, transferred the fish to a cup of milk. Naturally, within very little time, that lactose intolerant carp was belly up, much to Helen's great dismay. Her parents could only scratch their heads and ask, "What do you think you're doing?" Helen was scarred for life—and eschews dairy products, by the way.

When my son Ezra was two and a half, he gave me the fright of my life. One morning when I was doing dishes, he started crying. I looked over, and to my absolute horror, he had glued his eye shut with my nail glue. It was one of those moments when time and space just stand still. Instantly, I re-created the crime: Ez had supposed that my nail glue was eyedrops since it was in a similarly shaped bottle and, copying me, had dropped some glue in his eye. Mercy me! I was a mess, imagining emergency rooms and irreversibly damaged eyesight! I quickly washed his eye with a warm washcloth. Thankfully, the glue had not yet set and I was able to pry his eyelids open. *What was he thinking?* Well, I know what he was thinking, but still . . . wacky.

My friend Deone's daughter, Morgan, refused to wear anything other than a bathing suit for three months after her baby sister, Anna, was born. She would kick up a fuss like you wouldn't believe if other types of garments—say a dress for church—were introduced. Deone and her husband finally figured that this was Morgan's reaction to sharing them and her life with Anna. Morgan didn't have temper tantrums, or hide under the bed, or try and shove the baby off the couch like some older siblings have done. She simply wanted to wear a bathing suit every day. *That* she could control, somewhat, while the presence of a baby sister was completely out of Morgan's toddler hands. And just so you know, neither Morgan nor Anna is scarred for life. They get along famously, actually. During the bathing suit era, though, her actions just seemed nutty to everyone. "What in the world are you doing?" Deone probably wanted to ask her tyke as day after day the old bathing suit went on.

It would be nice to outgrow the mind-boggling folly of youth, but sometimes we adults still do things that make no sense to anyone, least of all ourselves. I look back on some of the actions I've taken and things I've said and wonder what in the world I was thinking. Putting a fish in milk, gluing an eye shut, and wearing a pink two-piece every day is kooky stuff, but it's all child's play compared to the sinful compulsions and ruts we grown-ups get ourselves into. Even the apostle Paul talked openly about how frustrating it was for him to do those things he knew he shouldn't do.

Just as the grown-ups in the lives of Helen, Ez, and Morgan could see, after a while, why their children had acted so bizarrely, so God knows our motivations, yearnings, and failures. He knows how our compulsive natures can sometimes act faster than our brains. But the difference is that he has given us the tools and support we need to stay on track, to not veer away from what we know is good and right and sane.

"If any of you lacks wisdom, [she] should ask God, who gives generously to all without finding fault, and it will be given to [her]," James writes (James 1:5). We have wisdom, boundless love, rock solid support from above, beneath, and beside us. We are "hemmed in" from every side, braced securely against every attack. We have angels fighting on our behalf and a God who died to cover our sins and give us power and strength. When we believe that deep down in the very core of our being, we will never again cause anyone, especially ourselves, to say, "What in the world are you doing?"

For what I do is not the good I want to do;
no, the evil I do not want to do—
this I keep on doing.

Romans 7:19

8: were you born in a barn?

How many are your works, O LORD!
In wisdom you made them all;
the earth is full of your creatures.

Psalm 104:24

Tallulah, our beautiful gray feline, *was* born in a barn, yet she could teach a Ph.D. in early childhood development a thing or two about mothering. Recently Tallulah gave birth to three kittens in Ezra's closet. That was her first act of motherhood, choosing a safe and cozy home for her litter.

Beforehand we judged by her lumpy middle and telltale waddle that Tallulah was going to make us Alpha Grandma and Grandpa. I fretted about where, when, and how she would give birth. Would we be up all night serving as midwives for our cat's delivery? I fretted about what could go wrong. *Nah,* said Doyle the farm boy. Animals do just fine all by themselves. He was right: Tallulah did not need me for a doula. We didn't even hear her give birth and only realized she had by the squeaks coming out of Ezra's closet.

First she had just one, a chip off the old block, gray with a slight striped pattern. One kitten? That didn't seem right. Indeed, cats always have more than one unless they have miscarried. And Tallulah still looked a bit lumpy. As I was a bit lumpy for quite some time after giving birth to my children, I thought that must be it: water weight gain. But no, eighteen hours or so after the first of the litter was born, Tallulah delivered two more kittens, a pair of black babies with white feet.

It's amazing to me how, without the benefit of *What to Expect When You're Expecting,* or an OB/GYN, or any help whatsoever, Tallulah was instantly a good mom. She cleaned her babies, kept them warm and safe, her eyes wide and alert if anyone, even her human family, came near. In fact, two days after the whole lot was born, Mama carried each kitten, one by one, down two flights of stairs to the basement, moving them to what she perceived as a safer den. I fretted some more: wouldn't those darling kittens be too cold down in the storage room? Again, Farm Boy spoke. "She will know if it's too cold," Doyle said. "Then she'll move them again if she has to." Two days later we heard squeaking in the middle of the night. Despite the mini cats' protests, Tallulah moved the whole kitten caboodle once more, this time to the hall closet.

So there sits Mother Cat tending to a brood of younguns. Sometimes she emerges from the closet and joins us in the outside world. Poor thing nurses all the livelong day! (Remember those marathon breastfeeding weeks, when it seemed like all you did was nurse?) She must feel more like a cow than a cat. I take my hat off to her. As a mom, Tallulah gives her little ones exactly what they need, no more and no less. She doesn't spoil them or feed them too much or too little. Innately, Tallulah knows how to feed her babies, care for them, protect them, and establish boundaries around their itty-bitty universe. She even has the instinct to get away from them once in a while, leaving them for a cuddle, a walk, or a long draft of milk.

Watching the cat family at our house has been like something on the Discovery Channel. We've had very interesting conversations about umbilical cords, breastfeeding, and how Tallulah came to have these kittens in the first place. "I think the kittens have more than one father," Doyle reported one day at dinner. Naturally that sparked no end of discussion, not to mention a kick under the table from me!

Sadly, we must give away two of the kittens because our house is not a four-cat type of dwelling. But for another couple of months, we have the wonderful opportunity to watch Tallulah's babies grow and change and to observe her natural knack for parenthood.

God's design is gloriously evident in his creatures. I marvel at the mother's intuition the Creator has wired into Tallulah. I wonder at the beauty and intricacy of three perfect kittens. I stand in awe at the work of his hands in nature and at how no detail is too small for his attention and care.

Are not two sparrows sold for a penny? Yet not one of them will fall to the ground apart from the will of your Father.

Matthew 10:29

9: don't make a mountain out of a molehill

You strain out a gnat but swallow a camel.

Matthew 23:24

There's nothing like the hormones of pregnancy to make a woman lose all perspective. Take, for example, my now famous "You don't know where the towels are?" freak-out session early in my second pregnancy.

First, let me say that Doyle is a truly phenomenal man when it comes to helping out around the house. If I'm running on a tight deadline, he will drop everything after work and take over dinner, run herd on Jonah, and basically keep the house quiet until whatever I am working on is done.

That having been said, I was, at the time I promised to tell you about, irritated that the house was in shambles and that he didn't seem to care. While we were eating dinner one night, Doyle left the table to wipe up a spill. He picked up a dish towel from the countertop instead of getting a clean one from the kitchen drawer. This is where things started to get strange (cue up music from *The Twilight Zone*). All I could think was, *He is so utterly unconcerned about how this house looks that he doesn't even know where the clean towels are!* Neon "tilt" lights flashed. Sparks flew. Smoke billowed. I began to cry, and hot tears streamed down my face as I screeched bloody murder about standards and neglect and towel storage policies. The poor man was stunned. The look on his face was pure deer-in-the-headlights.

I rushed upstairs in a maelstrom of righteous indignation. I huffed and I puffed—until about five minutes later when I felt like the biggest buffoon the world had ever known. Did I go downstairs, embrace my maligned husband, and apologize ever so sweetly? Not a chance. Like a jerk, I marinated in my pride for a good long while until I realized I had no option whatsoever but to say I was sorry. I apologized a lot during my pregnancies, and chances are you did too—or do apologize, present tense, if you're pregnant now. (PMS can also set off these kinds of "making a mountain out of a molehill" episodes.)

Why was I so ticked about something so inconsequential? Unfortunately, we all lose perspective and make mountains out of molehills, so to speak, more often than we'd like. We lose our focus on the things that truly are vital and fixate instead on minutia. This happens way too often in the church, where we nitpick each other's theological preferences, ministry choices, and worship style options, completely oblivious to our own arrogance and pride.

The Pharisees took this kind of narrow-minded censure and perfected it into an art form. In Matthew 23 Jesus raked these guys over the coals, critical of their habitual preoccupation with the molehills and not the mountains. "Woe to you, teachers of the law and Pharisees, you hypocrites!" he ranted. "You give a tenth of your spices—mint, dill, and cumin. But you have neglected the more important matters of the law—justice, mercy, and faithfulness. You should have practiced the latter, without neglecting the former" (v. 23). Their puffed up heads were obsessed with tithing 10 percent, even to the very last sprig of mint, which is not a bad thing in itself. Jesus says to do it. But they went off the rails when they got so caught up in counting bunches of dill that they totally ignored the bigger issues of character and obedience. I love Jesus's next zinger: "You blind guides!" he exclaimed, probably shaking his head in wonder. "You strain out a gnat but swallow a camel" (v. 24). I pray God will soften my heart and clear my vision, helping me to understand the difference between gnats and camels and to devote my priorities, energies, and brain power to the camels.

Oh, and speaking of strained gnats, yes, Doyle did forgive me about the towel incident, being the gracious guy he is. And he also knows exactly where the towels are. In fact, he always did.

For what I received I passed on to you as of first importance: that Christ died for our sins.

1 Corinthians 15:3

10: this is going to hurt me more than it's going to hurt you

As a man disciplines his son,
so the LORD your God disciplines you.

Deuteronomy 8:5

I woke up in the emergency room delirious from heavy-duty pain medication, babbling to the rather George Clooney–like ER doc checking me over. Doyle said it almost would have been funny if he hadn't been so worried about me. A couple of hours earlier my brakes had failed and I had whizzed through a red light at a busy intersection. A car broadsided me, and I ricocheted into a tree on the sidewalk.

It took the EMTs on the scene an hour to cut me out of the car with the jaws of life. When I first emerged from the car, I was covered in blood. Still, I was in much better shape than I appeared. My injuries were not life-threatening, though the accident could have been much worse. The upshot: one broken pelvis, one cracked tailbone, and a closed-head injury. But I knew my name and phone number, and I knew that Clinton was president when Dr. Clooney quizzed me.

Thankfully, I have no memory of the accident. Doyle, however, does. He was home when he heard a horrendous crash. His sixth sense proved right: it was my car he saw crumpled like a tin can when he emerged to see if his worst fears had proved correct. The worst of it was the agonizing hour he spent by my car waiting for me to be pulled out. He thought when he saw the condition of the car that I would surely be dead or, best-case scenario, paralyzed.

The accident scared us terribly. We felt as shaken as if we'd spent quality time in a cement mixer. Most of all, the two of us were profoundly grateful to be alive and together. Doyle says that when I was being transported in the ambulance and was going in and out of consciousness, I kept asking for him. "Where's Doyle? Is Doyle okay?" I blithered, not comprehending that he was right there holding my hand.

This just goes to show that the subconscious is a powerful thing. Somehow my innermost thoughts and feelings, the essence of my soul, really, knew the truth better than my conscious mind. See, previous to the accident, I hadn't been the most loving wife on the planet. We had been married for five years, and in the months preceding the accident, I had been unhappy, discontent, and critical of Doyle and especially of us as a couple. My linen-wearing, animal-loving, city slicker self wondered how I had ever chosen to be with this flannel-wearing, deer-hunting, redneck country boy. Then an ex-boyfriend suddenly materialized in my life again, and you know what they say about first loves—and greener grass. I was on a fast-track to crashing and burning everything I believed in.

At that point my loving, good Father gave me a serious dose of correction, a spiritual spanking, if you will, in the form of a car accident, that literally knocked some sense into my thick head. "Discipline is what happens when our loving Father steps in to lift us away from our own destructive and unfruitful pursuits," says Bruce Wilkinson in his book *Secrets of the Vine*. Undoubtedly, God used my car crash to divert me from my collision course and put me back on the right track. A broken pelvis is no picnic, I'll tell ya. Neither is a head injury, which incidentally left quite a scar on my forehead. I could have had the scar removed, but I wanted to keep it as a souvenir of God's dealing with me. That scar reminds me of God's loving intervention in my life, of how he saved my marriage and turned my life around completely. Just as he planned, the accident and the aftermath pruned my heart of dead wood and produced new growth and even new life: three months later, when my pelvis was healed (*ahem*), we conceived Jonah.

"No chastening seems to be joyful for the present, but grievous; nevertheless, afterwards it yields the peaceable fruit of righteousness," says Hebrews 12:11 (NKJV). The experience was painful, difficult, and wrenching, but I wouldn't trade it. That crash taught me that God loves me enough to correct me. He always acts out of love, and like Bruce Wilkinson says, "He only has abundance and joy in mind when he deals with our lives."

Whom the Lord loves He chastens.

Hebrews 12:6 NKJV

11: use your indoor voice

How gracious [God] will be when you cry for help! As soon as he hears, he will answer you.

Isaiah 30:19

"How do I get my young toddler to stop screeching?"

I get asked that a lot. Typically this screeching business commences around the fifteen-month mark and can be exasperating—and *loud.*

Jessica's little guy, fifteen-month-old Jacob, "has lungs that would make opera singers do a double take," says his mom. "This kid loves to make his presence known in malls where there is an echo. Just a loud yelp! We usually don't do much to stop it, since it is so random. We try to shush him, but he's not quite sure what that means yet."

We thought Ezra was part child, part banshee at this age. But no matter how frustrating and ear piercing it was to have him screech like that, we sensed that his hollering wasn't an act of rebellion or disobedience. As I researched the roots of toddler squawking, I discovered something fascinating: when toddlers scream like shrill birds of prey, they aren't angry or upset, they are simply exhibiting their intense desire to interact with their parents and those who love them best.

Kids groove on your attention, and a toddler this age will do just about anything to get it. Their verbal skills are limited. They can't say, "Hey Mom, look at me! Aren't I just the bomb?" But they can squeal to raise the roof. If you're in this parenting camp right now, your tot's screeching may land on your last nerve even if you're one of the most unruffled parents around.

I trolled the email boxes of friends and relatives, asking for tips from anyone whose ears had endured the bellows of their offspring. My cousin-in-law, Alanna, a salt-of-the-earth woman if ever there was one, came through with this solution:

> When Bennett was around fifteen months, he would sit in his high chair and scream, not because he was angry, but mostly because he was happy or impatient. And his scream was high pitched and ear splitting! At my wits' end, I tried out a piece of grandfatherly advice from a man I knew, and it ended up working like a charm and solving our toddler problem (that one, at least). The next time Bennett was shrieking, I held the back of his neck (for support) with one hand and gently covered his mouth with the other. Then, quietly and firmly, I said "No screaming" into his ear. It was a very soft-spoken method of discipline; there was nothing forceful or negative or scar-causing about it! I don't think Max (Bennett's big brother, then going on four) even noticed I was disciplining Bennett most of the time. After about a week or two, we noticed improvement, and some of the screaming had lessened. By about a month of using this routine, my toddler completely stopped screaming. Where I used to get frustrated by the noise and haul him out of the high chair for time out, this technique was far more effective, and I felt like I had much better control of my own emotions, therefore feeling like a "better mother"![4]

Alanna hit the nail on the head when she suspected Bennett's howling wasn't because he was angry or trying to be naughty.

Like Ez (and possibly your tyke), Bennett was just yelling to communicate on some primal level his wish to be heard and acknowledged.

Heeding your child's cry for attention is a good way to turn down the volume. Kneeling down to Ezra's pint-sized level and expressing my care and interest often silenced the screechies at my house. Like Alanna, I couldn't let his screams take over the house. But it helped to know my child wasn't trying to annoy me; he was attempting to get some good old-fashioned face time with me.

As adults, we still crave positive and focused interaction with those we love. And only God can truly meet that need in the deepest way. *Thank you, Father, that you hear my cries every time and that you know exactly why I'm crying out for you. Thank you for listening and for cupping my face in your mighty hands, looking me in the eye, and saying, "I love you, my child. Tell me what's on your mind."*

You will call, and the LORD will answer;
you will cry for help, and he will say: "Here am I."

Isaiah 58:9

12: don't cry over spilled milk

I am glad to boast about my weaknesses, so that
the power of Christ may work through me.

2 Corinthians 12:9 NLT

Got spilled milk? Of course you do! You probably assume I'll have a story about spilled milk to insert here, but I don't. Obviously, enough milk—and juice, water, pop, and other drinks—has spilled at our house to fill up many gallons. But instead of regaling my readers with an anecdote about slopped beverages and the longsuffering mother who mops them up, I decided to peek behind the cliché to get to the meat of the milk saying.

Who was the first mom to say, "Don't cry over spilled milk," and why did it catch on like it did? Spilled milk comes from a lack of coordination, it's a graceless and accidental misfire that ends up being an irritating blip on the family radar. Spills happen. And I think that's why the original *tsk-tsking*, finger-wagging, head-shaking mom told her tearful klutz to get a grip: it's embarrassing, annoying, and even uncomfortable if the milk ends up in your lap, but it's just spilled milk—no reason to get all worked up about it.

If you'll allow me a little stretch here, I'll tell you the story of a recent mistake I made, a mothering miscue that left me pink-cheeked with embarrassment, uncomfortable, and yes, way too worked up about it. Call it my own "spilled milk" episode.

It was car-pool day, and I dragged a particularly fractious Ez to go fetch his big brother at kindergarten. En route, I noticed Ez had stopped crabbing about whatever it was he was crabbing about. A peek in the rearview mirror revealed a conked-out crab blissfully snoozing.

I hauled my leaden three-year-old out of his seat and began lugging him down the street. *Nope. Too heavy.* I made a split-second decision to lock all the car doors, find a spot closer to the entrance, and make a quick dash inside for Jonah. After all, I justified, there were already all kinds of parents and kids milling around outside. It would be impossible for a potential kidnapper to jimmy the doors open and snatch my kid with all these people around. I would be five minutes in and out.

Lo and behold, a parking spot opened up just then right in front of the kindergarten exit. I checked my sleeping beauty. Out cold. Locking all the van doors, I briskly walked into the building and hurriedly gathered my usually poky flock of car-pool children plus Jonah (he's poky too). I didn't stop to chat with the teachers or view Gordie, the Mexican corn snake who lives in the kindergarten room. "Hurry guys. Let's go! C'mon, c'mon, c'mon!" I rushed my troops as best I could down the hallway, up the stairs, and out the door. That's when I saw Ezra, very much awake, hanging out the van window and engaging in witty repartee with passersby. In fact, he had rolled down all the windows. I had no idea he knew how.

I was mortified, especially when I saw the looks on some of the other parents' faces. What kind of mother lets her toddler hang out alone in a van with all the windows rolled down? He easily could have fallen out and cracked his head open on the sidewalk! Then I saw someone I knew from church, a mom whom I admired and liked. Embarrassed? Uncomfortable? Check. I grasped then that I should have just awakened Ezra and taken him into the school, as much of a hassle as it would have been. You know what they say about hindsight.

I didn't cry over my mistake, but I did obsess about it for a while. Why hadn't I predicted that Ezra might wake up? Why wasn't I more together? Pretty soon it was time to let go of my mistake. I was wasting time dwelling on it. Yes, I was preoccupied, and I had made a flawed judgment, which just goes to show that I'm human and error-prone, a clay vessel. Messing up is part of life. It reveals our limitations and makes us depend on the One who loves us no matter how much milk we spill.

So I wouldn't get a big head, I was given the gift of a handicap to keep me in constant touch with my limitations.

2 Corinthians 12:7 Message

13: look on the bright side, dear

For our light and momentary troubles are achieving for us an eternal glory that far outweighs them all.

2 Corinthians 4:17

Moms are pros at finding silver linings. Even if our own temperament is more "glass half empty," we mothers are regular Pollyannas when it comes to helping our kids see the positive side of life.

"I know you're disappointed about losing the T-ball game, but look on the bright side: you made a new friend!"

"Yes, you spilled purple juice all over your horse picture, but that's okay, because now we can get a fresh piece of paper and make an even better picture."

"It's sad that Christopher is moving away, but won't it be great to visit him at his new house with a pool?"

We are relentless in hunting for silver linings in every little gray cloud that threatens to rain on our child's parade. Why do we so accentuate the positive? Because we hate to see our little men and women disappointed, sad, frustrated, or lonely. But as children of God, we know that these not-so-perfect experiences are what build character. We grow from failure and stretch after a setback. Everything that happens to us has spiritual significance.

It's hard to remember that, isn't it? I'm ridiculously sanguine about life most of the time. "When Life Gives You Lemons, Make Lemonade" is a bumper sticker just waiting to get slapped on the back of my minivan (that and "Hang Up and Drive!"). But even I am sometimes at a loss about the purpose of pain in my life and in the lives of others. My mom's bout with depression is one painful occurrence in my family's history that seemed to be all cloud.

I was in my mid-twenties when my mom first sank into a deep clinical depression. She literally woke up one morning and couldn't get out of bed. Dozens of visits to doctors followed, and dozens more medications were prescribed. Nothing, it seemed, was making any impression on the black shroud that cocooned her spirit. My mom was among the 20 percent of depression patients who are treatment resistant; that is, they don't respond to antidepressants. She also didn't respond to spiritual curatives. Countless prayers were submitted on her behalf, begging God to heal her, but her condition only got worse.

For my family, it was as if our real wife and mother had died and was replaced with this foreign woman who looked like Linda Reimer but certainly didn't act like her. Instead of bustling around the house turbo-cleaning and laughing, she would slump in her chair or in bed, lethargic, weepy, and indifferent to everyone and everything. Instead of being our sympathetic ear when things went wrong or our cheerleader when things went right, my mom could barely fake an interest in any of us. This apathy particularly hurt me when I became a mom myself. Visions I harbored for years, of calling my mom with breathless reports of my baby's latest and greatest milestone, were dashed.

My mom couldn't get excited about Jonah achieving the pincer grasp or anything else; she was too busy trying to survive. Such was her despair that she often was suicidal. At times I was filled with dread when the phone would ring, sure it would be my dad telling me my mom had ended her life. The fear of that hung around my neck like an albatross, heavy and wearisome.

Finally, after more than six years, my mom came back to us. A combination of many shock therapy treatments—they sound barbaric but are painless and very effective—and the right medication worked.

During those years, I would have been hard pressed to find a bright side. But when I started writing books and speaking to gatherings of young moms, I finally found one: I could tell women suffering from postpartum depression that they were not bad Christians, and that they could find help. My compassion for them ran deep, especially after I went through a time of PPD myself after Ezra was born. Several moms told me that they sought help for their depression after they read my books or listened to me talk about it. "Everything that happens to a child of God is *Father-filtered,"* says Rick Warren in *The Purpose-Driven Life*. God filtered my mom's years of mental illness through his good purpose and produced in me increased depth, closeness with him, and an empathy that has helped others find their own bright sides.

Because of the LORD's great love we are not consumed,
for his compassions never fail. They are new every morning.

Lamentations 3:22–23

14: don't make me stop this car!

Be content with what you have,
because God has said, "Never will I leave you;
never will I forsake you."

Hebrews 13:5

Do you ever feel as if you were placed on this earth to drive a minivan—everywhere? Let me back up. How many of you ever vowed you would never drive a minivan? Let's see a show of hands, please. Uh-huh. I thought so. Yet, unless you are very, very strong in your anti-minivan stance or have only one child, you probably caved in and got one about the time you were ready to give birth to your second child.

I love cars, especially European cars, which isn't exactly a popular position here in Michigan, where everybody and their uncle works in the automotive industry. My hope was that the only van-type vehicle I would ever drive would be a VW van, you know, one of those cool hippie-mobiles. The only problem is, those cost about twice what we could comfortably afford.

And my husband is from Michigan, which makes him kind of itchy on the whole idea of buying a foreign-made car.

So three years ago, right before Ezra was born, we found a two-year-old dark green Dodge Caravan with 28,000 miles. Sometimes you just have to be practical, which is one of the harder life lessons for an impractical woman like me. A Dodge Caravan? Not exactly the suave, global make I had envisioned as a teenage girl, who, I must say, had no clue as to the realities of car payments, mortgages, and groceries. Still, those visions from girlhood have a way of really sticking.

The color wasn't very exciting, either. I was kind of hoping for something prettier, like aqua and silver, or cerulean, or bronze. Some chick color. Do you know how many dark green Dodge Caravan minivans there are? They are a dime a dozen, crawling over every mall, supermarket, and school parking lot in the western hemisphere.

But God had seen fit to provide an unexciting, uncool, and un-cerulean minivan for our family. It was a great value—the dealer had knocked off a thousand dollars from the price quoted on his webpage. Other vans of the same vintage and cost had 30,000 to 60,000 miles on their odometers. Undoubtedly, God was cutting us a deal.

Right off the bat, as my pregnant self helped buckle my three-year-old into his car seat, I knew we had done the right thing. It was infinitely easier to accomplish the car-seat routine without having to bend and crane and twist and . . . you get the idea. And when we added another car seat soon after? We were thrilled with the space and ease of double sliding doors.

Many of you know where I'm headed with this tale of woman meets van. I soon fell head over heels in locomotion love with that boring green machine. I looked up its safety rating on the Internet: very good in its class, the report said. And minivans have significantly fewer incidents of rollovers than those chic, exciting, cerulean SUVs out there.

None of us realizes, when we are pregnant with our first child, just how much raising of that child and those to follow will take place in the family auto. We log thousands of miles of life together in our mundane minivan—from short, routine trips to church, the doctor's office, Grandma's house, preschool, playdates, and soccer, hockey, and T-ball games, to lengthy road trips, including a thousand miles home to Winnipeg, a thousand-plus to South Carolina to see Uncle Mike graduate from college, and four hundred round-trip to Chicago once a year or more.

We taught our kids the words to "O Canada," "The Star-spangled Banner," and "God Save the Queen," all our collective national anthems, in that van. We rocked out to the radio, told jokes, and passed countless Happy Meals from front to back. This summer we plan a road trip to Quebec, about fourteen hours as the crow flies. I'm scouting the local bookstore for a CD/book program I saw once: "Learn French in the Car." Even if we don't drive the most exotic car in the world, we can pick up a foreign language while we're driving!

How do I answer that disapproving teenage girl inside me who thinks I have sold out my true self? First, I tell her our "true self" couldn't afford the car payments, and no, we didn't actually marry a rich hockey player from Finland. Then I tell her to count her blessings and never look a gift horse—or horse-power—in the mouth.

Every good and perfect gift is from above.

James 1:17

15: say cheese!

Let love and faithfulness never leave you;
bind them around your neck,
write them on the tablet of your heart.
Proverbs 3:3

Are you a snap-happy mom? I'm definitely guilty of that charge. I love to take shots of my kids doing just about anything and everything. Playing, lounging, potty training (you have to have a few naked baby pictures on hand to mortify your child's first boyfriend or girlfriend, don't you think?), eating—nothing is off limits to Mom and her kamikaze camera. Why? Because scrapbooking is addictive. I found myself signing my son up for T-ball because those baseball die-cuts and stickers are so dang cute—oh, and also he wanted to play T-ball.

Lisa Whelchel, of *Facts of Life* fame and also the author of several great books on motherhood, confessed how her urge to crop can be overwhelming at times. "I have to admit I have taken my role as family photohistorian to extremes," she writes in her book *The Facts of Life: And Other Lessons My Father Taught Me*. Lisa tells how, one Christmas, her husband, Steve, fell off the roof putting icicle lights up. The poor man lay motionless on the ground, the victim of two broken arms and one broken leg. "When I tell you what I did next, please cut me some slack. I went into the house and got my camera. I took pictures of the paramedics checking Steve's vital signs, strapping him onto the board, and putting him into an ambulance." (All of you cropaholics out there are nodding your head in understanding. What else is to be done but take pictures at a time like that?)

But Lisa's little daughter, Haven, was horrified. "Mommy, how could you take pictures *now*?" At least one person understood—the paramedic taking care of Steve. "He took one look at me clicking away and said, 'Scrapbooker?'" Lisa made her infirm husband say "cheese" throughout the entire trial, beginning her click-a-thon in the ER and working her way through X-rays, the wheelchair days, the leg brace, and on and on. She snapped Steve going into surgery, working with his physical therapist, and finally going back to work.

Why did she document her husband's mishap so thoroughly? For a scrapbook, silly! Ultimately all the pics filled eight scrapbook pages that were accompanied by a lengthy journal section detailing the whole story of how the Lord miraculously saved Steve's life and protected him every step of the way. "It's a written reminder of the Lord moving in the life of our family and will be a testimony to our children and grandchildren and great-grandchildren," Lisa writes.[5]

This story made me laugh at both Lisa's zeal and my own. It also challenged me to consider the art of scrapbooking in a different way. As Lisa points out, we won't be able to photograph some of our encounters with the Lord. But we can write the stories down, not only to remind ourselves of those times, but also as a witness to the generations of family that follow. Like Abraham, Noah, Isaac, Moses, Gideon, Saul, David, and other Bible Hall of Famers who built altars to commemorate the Lord's workings and interactions with them, we can craft our own "altars" with photos and stickers and die-cuts. The most important element to such an altar would obviously be the journaling, recording the stories of our lives so those we love can be blessed and uplifted by them.

Chatting, laughing, eating, and cropping. What could be better? Just one thing: in addition to our adorable photos of our little men and women up to bat, blowing out candles, and spit-shined and gleaming in Easter clothes, we can chronicle their faith journeys and ours. Archiving God's interactions with us may not fit as neatly as T-ball into a sticker theme, but it will leave a heritage for the next generation. If acid-free scrapbook pages stand the test of time, our scrapbooks will stand as altars, testimonies to God's faithfulness in meeting our needs—and meeting us.

Fix these words of mine in your hearts and minds. . . .
Write them on the doorframes of your houses and on your gates.

Deuteronomy 11:18, 20

16: if johnny jumps off a cliff, are YOU going to jump too?

So then, let us not be like others, who are asleep, but let us be alert and self-controlled.

1 Thessalonians 5:6

In the movie *13 Going on 30*, a young teenager, Jenna (played by Jennifer Garner), thinks her life stinks because she's not as cool as the Six Chicks tribe of she-wolves who rule her school. Though Jenna wishes she were in the hip crowd, her actual best friend is Matt, her chubby, decidedly uncool neighbor who obviously thinks she's the best thing since Twinkies. Of course, his crush is unrequited.

Jenna laments her flat chest, metal mouth, and low placement on the social food chain. Inspired by an article in her favorite magazine, *Poise*, entitled "Thirty, Flirty, and Thriving," Jenna latches on to the idea that to be thirty is to have it all and then some. When her thirteenth birthday party goes horribly wrong, Jenna makes a birthday wish to be thirty. Voila! The next morning, Jenna awakens in a fabulous New York City apartment, her thirty-year-old life complete with a walk-in closet and a studmuffin hockey player boyfriend.

Surprises abound for the fish out of water. For example, she is now best friends with Lucy, the queen snob of the cruel Six Chicks clique from middle school. Jenna also discovers to her dismay that she isn't a very nice thirty-year-old: underlings at work are scared of her, and she is completely out of touch with Matt. And when she does find her long-lost best buddy, he has grown into a handsome, gentle, endearing guy (surprise, surprise).

If you have seen the movie, you know that eventually Lucy's true colors show, and she is revealed to be just as warped and self-centered and mean-spirited as she was in middle school.

This particular film isn't supposed to be profound, but oddly enough my girlfriends and I found it to be so. (Maybe we need to get out more!) What resonated with us is that Jenna wanted so badly to be like Lucy and the Six Chicks that she would change her personality and interests and even hurt her truest friend to assimilate. Her story illustrates how powerful the temptation to fit in can be. With her new thirty-year-old perspective, Jenna could see with crystal clarity that Lucy and her ilk weren't worth bending over backwards to be like them. To stretch it a bit, Jenna's fierce desire to be liked caused her to sin, turning her back on Matt and morphing into a conceited she-wolf herself.

My friends and I lingered by our cars for quite a while, talking about our own rather hideous junior high experiences and how at that age we would have gladly sold our souls to be accepted by certain groups. Why had we all been so skewed by the allure of popularity? One of our group, Cindy, recalled how she had been shunned one day for no apparent reason other than she had been away from school during the time when her friends formed a "club" without her. Someone had read in a book that five was the perfect number for a girl's club, and since Cindy would make six, she was cut off from their friendship. For three years she suffered from the humiliation of being on the outside looking in. Then suddenly one day she was back "in," as if nothing had ever happened. Another woman told how she too had been avoided, ignored, and whispered about during her eighth-grade year by a powerful girl's clique. It hurt like crazy when it was going on, she said, but ultimately her pain and loneliness as a social outcast led her straight into the arms of her heavenly Father.

My sons are still small, yet even they have experienced to some degree the forces of peer pressure. Jonah is so socially motivated, so into being part of the gang, that I fear for him. He has already made comments about other boys seeing certain movies, playing with certain toys, and even wearing a particular type of clothing. "Just because so and so does this doesn't mean you have to," I tell him, my parents' words echoing in my mind. I pray my son will have the courage and character to follow his own path even if it means he won't be liked at times. I too want to be liked by other people. I'm a "pack animal" who loves people and groups. But, like Jenna, I have come to realize that being accepted and adored by people is a fleeting thing. Being accepted and adored by God is a given, now and for eternity.

Be strong and courageous.
Do not be terrified; do not be discouraged,
for the Lord your God will be with you wherever you go.
Joshua 31:9

17: i don't care who started this

For in the same way you judge others,
you will be judged, and with the measure
you use, it will be measured to you.

Matthew 7:2

Sheri gave birth to her first baby and was eager to nurse him. She had read all about the benefits of breastfeeding and wanted nothing less than the best for her firstborn. But, despite the many lectures and tips from lactation consultants at the hospital, Sheri was unable to breastfeed Jacob properly. She tried various holds and attempted a number of techniques for getting the itty-bitty boy to open his mouth wide and latch on. And she spent precious time on the phone talking with lactation consultants. One or two of these milking mentors even stopped by her house to show her how it's done. Still, nothing worked, and Sheri gave up. She was disappointed that breastfeeding hadn't worked for her, but she felt good about simply feeding her son with a bottle in a relaxed manner without the stress and tears of trying to figure out nursing.

A few weeks later a friend who had given Sheri a book on nursing as a baby gift asked how breastfeeding was going. When Sheri detailed all the methods she had tried and the help she had employed—to no avail—the friend's eyes narrowed with disbelief. "Did you try the football hold?" she asked. Yes, Sheri had tried it. "The cradle?" Check. "Cross-cradle?" Check, check. The friend went on to quiz Sheri on her efforts at every hold and maneuver known to lactation science. After a while, the friend's questions started to sound more like an interrogation, and Sheri was left with the distinct impression that this "pal" was sorely disappointed.

At this same get-together, Sheri overheard her friend whispering about her behind her back. "She obviously didn't try hard enough," the woman *tsk-tsked*. "Well, she's going to miss out on the best part of motherhood. It's really such a shame." Sheri was hurt, baffled, and indignant. She had exerted all kinds of effort to try to nurse her baby. In her mind, she knew she had exhausted every avenue in her quest to breastfeed. And yet her so-called friend had passed judgment on her for not trying hard enough (subtext: Sheri was a bad mommy).

The friendship hit the skids and never really recovered. Sheri couldn't get past her friend's smug attitude and, worse, the woman's indictment of her mothering skills. Very little hurts as much as a negative judgment of the way we raise our children. Often, the critiquing begins before we even give birth. Before I had my second C-section (a car accident years before had likely produced scar tissue in my pelvis, and my doctor advised a scheduled cesarean), a woman at my church clucked and shook her head in disapproval when Doyle told her about my plans. "I just don't think that's wise," she told him. Well, we rolled our eyes and paid no heed, but of course I became more wary in my encounters with her.

Bottle versus breast. Scheduling versus feeding on cue. Working or staying at home. These debates can get as hot as any contentious scuffle on the floor of the state legislature. And they are just the beginning of a lifetime of choices we make as moms that pit us against another group who is making the opposite choice. What adds heat to our decisions is our great love for our children and our intense commitment to be the best moms we can be. If our friend chooses differently than us, we can take that to be an accusation that our own views on the matter are wrong, and vice versa. *If I let my kids eat hot dogs, and she doesn't, that must mean she thinks I'm lax and don't care as much about my kids as she does.* Sadly, this type of friction has come between many mommy friends.

The longer I'm a mother, the more I see that we moms need to be each other's cheerleaders. We all have issues that, for whatever reason, are vital to our mothering, but to impose our standards and choices on other moms is shortsighted and selfish. Instead of judging, we need to adopt a "live and let live" attitude about other moms and focus on our own efforts to be the women and mothers God called us to be.

Why do you look at the speck of sawdust in your brother's eye and pay no attention to the plank in your own eye?

Matthew 7:3

18: you're not leaving the house dressed like that!

For he has clothed me with garments
of salvation and arrayed me in a
robe of righteousness.

Isaiah 61:1

"Jonah!" I was utterly agog at my six-year-old boy, who was at that moment crawling under the minivan for some unfathomable reason. It was Easter Sunday morning, a crisp, sunny day befitting the celebration of Christ's resurrection. The night before, I had laid out all kinds of cute shirts, pants, socks, and vests for my menfolk, big and small.

Sometimes on a Sunday morning, I must admit, we run around looking for suitable socks and decent, reasonably clean tops or bottoms to complete our ensembles, but not on that Sunday. Jonah was a sharply dressed little man in his shirt, vest, and matching pants, with his cowlicks slicked down and his face unusually clean. How handsome my boy had become, how grown-up, all duded-up in his new finery! My motherly pride was running high that morning.

But the words *proud* and *handsome* were the last ones on my brain as I was confronted with the sight of three-quarters of my firstborn's body submerged under the van.

"What in the world are you doing?" I hollered, my eyes wide and my jaw dropped in astonishment. "Get out from under the car right now!"

Neighbors were starting to stare, or at least that's the notion that suddenly flitted through my paranoid brain. Not that I cared too much what my neighbors thought, although I always tried to model Christ in my interactions with them. Now I was yelling at my child—on Easter Sunday! And I still had no clue what would possess my child to dive onto the dirty ground under the van.

"I was just trying to get Ezra's ball!" Jonah had started to cry, sensing at once that his roll in the dirt wasn't such a hot idea. His pants were stained with grass and mud from the knees up. The stylin' Easter outfit was toast.

Doyle chose that moment to emerge from the house. "Jonah, go change your pants!" was his contribution to the situation. Through gritted teeth, I explained that, for spring dress-up pants that would fit the kid, the stained pants were it. (You moms know exactly how it is when a new season comes along and you suddenly realize your child has outgrown every seasonal piece of clothing from last year. Which is why I had the savvy foresight, of course, to buy the child new pants!) Doyle is a great husband and dad, but fashion conscious he is not. No doubt he would have gone back in the house and grabbed the first pair of pants he saw. Too short? Too tight? Clashing colors? Doyle wouldn't have registered such details as being important. Pants are pants in his mind.

Naturally, in my mind, pants are much more than pants. You and I both know they are a key component to the overall sartorial presentation. My fashion diagnosis was grim: it was too cold for shorts, too warm for heavy corduroy pants, and too formal for jeans. There was no solution other than to have Jonah wear his muddy trousers to church.

Jonah, blotchy-faced and somber, was upset about this, embarrassed and chagrined about the state of his attire. I was still in shock that somehow I had failed to impart a "no crawling under the car with clean clothes" statute. Doyle was irritated that we were now going to be late for church, but he found it in himself to take a stab at humor: "Why don't we all roll around on the ground?" he asked. "That way we'll all match."

Hardy har har. Well, we were a subdued clan who filed into church that morning, hardly the cheerful troupe of holiday merrymakers we had been earlier when the boys were exulting over their Easter baskets. But by the second or third worship song, my feelings of annoyance began to melt away. Clothes and looks have always been important to me, and I guess I will always enjoy putting together colors and designs. Yes, my son was wearing grubby pants, but who cares? My attitude was as stained and skewed as his outfit, I realized. I almost let a mishap with muddy clothes take my eyes off the One who lived and died and rose to dress me in salvation and righteousness.

She is clothed with strength and dignity.

Proverbs 31:25

19: "sticks and stones may break your bones . . ."

Fix these words of mine into
your hearts and minds.

Deuteronomy 11:18

My friend Sheri was told by a high school guidance counselor that she wasn't college material. Disheartened, Sheri nonetheless went on to attain both her bachelor's and master's degrees in social work. Still, her counselor's words sometimes haunt her. *What did she see in me that made her think I wasn't cut out for college?* she wonders.

Rachel excelled as a high school English teacher. Her enthusiasm for classic literature bubbled over into her teaching, and her students loved Miss Vanderlaan's energy and dry humor. But in college Rachel had been told by her advising professor that she shouldn't pursue teaching English. "You don't have what it takes," the professor said. "You won't be good at teaching English." Obviously, my friend proved her professor wrong, going on to inspire and mold young minds.

Though it's a wonderful feeling to justify her career choice, Rachel wonders once in a while why this professor was so sure she should take up turnip farming or metallurgy—anything but teaching English.

Words can hurt you badly. They can even shape your future if you believe them. Had Sheri and Rachel believed their teachers' negative words, neither would have enjoyed the satisfaction and rewards of their chosen vocations. Both were devastated by the shattering words spoken by "authorities." But both my friends also trusted something deeper than the assessments of their teachers: themselves, and more vital, God's words to them about their worth, their gifts, and their potential.

I worked in a women's clothing store for about six months between high school and college. My boss was a scrawny, chain-smoking fashionista who intimidated me to no end. She and her friends were worldly and sophisticated, and they seemed to look down on people like me as being naïve, dull, and not too swift.

One day this woman, Michelle, and I were working alone. I was steaming dresses and pantsuits while she waited to pounce on the next customer who darkened our door. Maybe she was bored, but all of a sudden she pounced on me. "Lori, I know what you should do with your life!" She scurried over to me, eyes wide with enthusiasm.

A little background: I had shyly shared with Michelle and company a dream of mine to go to college and obtain a broadcasting degree, launching me, hopefully, onto CNN or NBC, something like that. (Actually, I would have gladly read news for a station in Fargo, North Dakota, but a dream is a dream!) I had felt shy about divulging this, not only because I was slightly scared (okay, scared spitless) of Michelle and my other arcane co-workers, but because Michelle's "best friend" was a well-known television journalist in our city. ("Best friend" my elbow!)

Whenever this man would come visit her, I was awed by his oh-so-journalistic presence. To me, Michelle's friendship with the quasi-famous dude made her, by association, an authority on broadcast journalism. So I wasn't exactly overjoyed with her next words:

"You're just so sweet and adorable and all—you should write romance novels!" Michelle was obviously thrilled with her suggestion, but as she stood there beaming at me, something precious inside my soul crumpled like a fender impacted by a Mack truck.

"Really?" I said, trying to disguise my huge disappointment.

"Oh yeah! You'd be perfect. I don't think you have the 'animal instinct' to be on TV, but I could see you making a million writing romantic stories."

Wonderful. My dream of me in a power suit interviewing presidents and famous felons went *poof,* and in its place came a picture of me in puffed sleeves pecking away at my keyboard, concocting fluffy cotton candy stories of Fabio and Cherish's sweet and adorable romance. I took the disappointment to heart, and it took me a while to wriggle my way out of the cage of Michelle's opinion. When the dust settled, I realized that Michelle—"expert" or not—was only one person. I prayed and felt God was still leading me to be a broadcasting major and have a journalism career. He had given me a passion for it, and until I heard differently—from him—I would continue on that path.

Ironically, Michelle was partly right. In the real world, I would have lacked that "going-for-the jugular" dynamic all great TV journalists have. Feature writing for magazines and newspapers is the kind of journalism I am good at. And as a true romantic, if I ever write those novels burning in my bosom, I'm sure a few three-hankie mushy stories will emerge in the plots.

The upshot? God does work through people, helping us learn about ourselves from their views and opinions of who we are. But his words should always mean the most to us. Our Father's perspective of our value as his daughters, our talents, our journey, should always be our North Star, guiding us each step of the way.

My sheep listen to my voice.

John 10:27

20: just because i love you, that's why

God will generously provide all you need.
Then you will always have everything you need
and plenty left over to share with others.

2 Corinthians 9:8 NLT

Sabrina was prepared to shell out up to a thousand dollars for a wedding dress. She was among oodles of brides-to-be rummaging through the deeply discounted bridal gowns at the "Brides for Breast Cancer" benefit at a local hotel. (Recent brides donate their gowns, worn only once of course, to the benefit, which sells the beauties at a substantially lower price than what they are worth. Proceeds are donated to breast cancer research.)

Unbeknown to Sabrina, a senior citizen named Peter had also stopped by the benefit to quietly pay tribute to his own daughter, who had died of cancer a year and a half before. "I want to buy a wedding dress for the seventeenth woman to go through the checkout," he whispered to a benefit organizer, adding that his donation was intended to honor the memory of his child, Carol Sue. Seventeen was simply his favorite number. Peter wrote a check for six hundred dollars and left with tears in his eyes.

Sabrina approached the checkout, having found the dress of her dreams. The benefit organizer had been counting, and Sabrina was number seventeen. "A beautiful dress," she told the young woman, "and it's yours at no cost."

As the explanation for her windfall unfolded, Sabrina herself was brought to tears, not only by a stranger's generosity, but also by the depth of feeling behind Peter's gesture. Sabrina's dress would be imbued with so much more than beads and lace and appliqués; it would represent a loving and sweet memorial to a much-loved woman who was once Peter's little girl.

Sabrina also experienced a frisson of connection to heaven, where her own beloved aunt, a victim of cancer, now resided. Thoughts of her aunt Alice, a big fan of weddings, had been close by as Sabrina had searched for her gown. She was convinced that somehow her aunt had pulled a few strings for her earthbound niece.

When Peter had read about the Brides for Breast Cancer benefit in the newspaper, he had felt nudged to pay tribute to Carol Sue in this way and bring a little joy to someone else's heart. That heart was Sabrina's, who days after the benefit was still in awe of her beautiful dress and the special, meaningful way in which she had come to own it. She was able to share her gratitude with Peter soon after when the local newspaper, which had learned about Sabrina's story, photographed a beaming bride-to-be and her benefactor.

Undoubtedly, both Sabrina and Peter were blessed and heartened by this meeting, two strangers whose acquaintance was precipitated by one's unselfish act of grace and generosity. I hoped Sabrina and her fiancé would invite Peter to their summer wedding so that he could witness firsthand the radiance of a young bride dressed in his gift.

It struck me that Sabrina did nothing to deserve a free wedding dress. She didn't even buy a lottery ticket or enter a raffle to win a dress. The schoolteacher was fully intending to pay for her dress with her own money, but just because she was number seventeen, she came away with a surprise blessing and a million-dollar memory.

This story reminded me that, as God's child, I am the recipient of his blessings, his acts of grace and mercy, and his favor every day.

Let's be awake to the many blessings God our Father gifts us with, his sweet and wonderful surprises. Let's be grateful we have such a generous, gracious Savior, who gave us the ultimate gift of his salvation even though we didn't do a thing to deserve it.

A gift opens the way for the giver and
ushers him into the presence of the great.
Proverbs 18:16

21: tuck in your shirt

Consider how the lilies grow.
They do not labor or spin.

Luke 12:27

"Your shirt is kind of wrinkled," the intimidating TV producer said to me, her own nose wrinkled with disapproval as I sat in the makeup chair having foundation applied to my face. "Oh, really? I ironed it about fifteen minutes ago," I said in as pleasant a tone as I could muster. What I really wanted to say was something more snide, like, "Look, lady, if you knew what I went through to get this shirt, you'd congratulate me for being clothed period!"

Let me back up a little. I was in Dallas one smoking hot September morning when this little exchange took place. Late afternoon on the day before, I left Grand Rapids, kissing my family good-bye with the calm assurance that within a few hours I would be unpacking my clothes in a Dallas hotel room. That weekend I was to appear on two television shows to promote one of my books. Naturally I was nervous, because it's not every day I'm on TV, and I was hoping it would go well and I wouldn't say anything ridiculous or have a coughing fit or fall off my chair. Okay, so I'm a little neurotic.

My trip was not nearly that simple. First of all, my flight from Grand Rapids was grounded for an hour for iffy weather, which meant I missed my connecting flight in Detroit. The airline people rebooked me on a circuitous route that would take me all over tarnation before eventually getting back to Dallas. Irritated and a bit weary already, I phoned home in Memphis, only to receive the terrible news that my beloved uncle Al's cancer had spread from his liver to his bones. My beautiful young uncle, more like an older brother than an uncle, was one of my closest friends and a precious confidant. He probably wouldn't make it after all, though we'd had a glimmer of hope he might. The news was shattering, but I knew I had to hold it together, at least until the following afternoon when the first TV show was over.

All the way to Dallas I cried and prayed and cried some more. It was one o'clock a.m. by the time I got to Texas, heartsick and makeup bawled clean off my face. If I could get to my downtown hotel in the next half-hour, I could get about six hours of sleep, I reckoned.

There was only one problem: my luggage was lost. You savvy frequent fliers out there are shaking your heads, I know. But all my stuff, including two great new "TV" outfits, makeup, even directions to the TV station, were floating around in Timbuktu or Topeka—certainly nowhere near Dallas.

It was now the middle of the night, no stores were open, my luggage was MIA, and I had to be on my first ever network-affiliate TV show in seven hours.

I cracked. Between the distressing news about my uncle and the fact that I was facing the prospect of promoting a Christian book in the nude, I just kind of fell to pieces right there in the luggage room at Dulles Airport. *Lord God, get me through this and get me some clothes—puh-lease!*

The situation seemed very grim indeed. Where, oh where, would I find something suitable to wear in a strange city in the middle of the night? "But I have to be on TV tomorrow morning and I don't have any clothes!" I blubbered to the rather severe woman (she looked like a prison matron, actually) behind the lost luggage counter. She probably thought, *Yeah right, this chick is going on TV like I'm entering the Miss America pageant!* Still, her hard features softened ever so slightly, and the words she barked at me next were straight from the throne room of grace: "Why don't cha go to the all-night Wal-Mart?"

"Wal-Mart is open all night?" I said, stupefied by this newsflash. Not in Grand Rapids they aren't, but—Thank you, Lord!—in the great state of Texas they are.

Before you could say, "Remember the Alamo," I was in a cab being driven to the nearest twenty-four-hour Wal-Mart by a kind, understandably confused young cabbie named Rasheed. "Rasheed," I begged as he dropped me off at Wal-Mart, "please just wait here while I find what I need!" Racing around like some kind of suburban Tasmanian devil woman, I grabbed a powder blue shirt and dress pants and made like a bandit for the checkout. By the time I got back to blessed, wonderful Rasheed and his cab, I was panting, spent by my frenzied shopping trip.

That night I got four hours of sleep, but I arrived at the TV station on time, garbed in my brand-new blue shirt from Wal-Mart. True, it wrinkled the minute I sat down, but my upper body was covered, and that's all I cared about right then. God literally supplied me with the shirt on my back, against all odds, and I know he is faithful to provide me with exactly what I need.

My God will meet all your needs according to his glorious riches in Christ Jesus.

Philippians 4:19

22: YOU can do it!

It is God who arms me with strength
and makes my way perfect.
He makes my feet like the feet of the deer;
he enables me to stand on the heights.

Psalm 18:32–33

"You can do it, Keri!" Coach Bela Karolyi urged his tiny protégée, Keri Strug, who gritted her teeth, summoned all her moxie, and stuck her second vault after injuring her ankle on her first attempt moments earlier. *"You can do it, Keri!"* She could, and she did! Keri's grit and determination captured the attention of the watching world. It was 1996, the peak of the Summer Olympic Games in Atlanta. Has it been almost a decade since this pint-sized heroine catapulted herself, sprained ankle and all, to the USA's first team gold medal in gymnastics? What a moment that was, as this eighteen-year-old girl fought through excruciating pain to secure the shimmering prize for her team.

Of course, gold medals and American pride aside, Keri's coaches, Karolyi and his wife, Martha, drew fire for allowing (i.e., pushing) the girl to execute the high-priced second vault. After all, Keri had suffered two torn ligaments and a sprained ankle that would force her out of the rest of the games. The whole episode raised quite a brouhaha about how far athletes should be pushed.

Yes, it was an incredible moment, grace under pressure personified by the Herculean gymnast. But I'm with the critics. If I were Keri Strug's mom, I would have thrown myself bodily in front of hefty Bela myself to stop him from pushing my child to brutalize her body that way—gold medal or not.

For some quirky reason, though, Doyle and I have continued to use "You can do it," mimicking Bela Karolyi's thick Romanian accent, as a half-joking, half-serious catchphrase when one of us is called upon to go out on a limb. We say it to our kids too, who don't get the joke and think once again that the old folks at their house are a bit odd. Still, we say it and we mean it. Our kids need some *rah, rah, rah!* coaching once in a while to hurdle their own insecurities and perceived limitations.

"I'm no good at art," Jonah sighed one day, his little shoulders slumped in discouragement. How many hours had the two of us logged, elbow-deep in glue, paint, clay, before school even started? Too many for my pint-sized Picasso to throw in the towel in kindergarten.

"Honey, that's not true. You draw really well. Why would you say you're no good at art?"

"I just couldn't do my collage. It looked ugly and weird," he said. I assured him it probably didn't look ugly and weird, but he insisted it did. Actually, Jonah soon lost interest in the conversation while his mom continued to stew over it for quite a while. I finally deduced, that for that particular art project, he hadn't been satisfied with the results. Probably, whatever technique the art teacher (a good one, by the way) had introduced was challenging to him, and he felt discouraged when it hadn't turned out as perfectly as he would have liked.

A challenge, though, is a good thing. Life is full of challenges, one of them being ours as mothers to continually spur our kids to do their best and not get beaten down by hurdles, difficulty, and discouragement. It starts when we are trying to get our babies to roll over or sit up or take their first tottering steps. "You can do it!" we cheer with all the gusto in our proud mother selves. This mommy coaching stuff gets even harder when our babies grow up and face trials at school, on the playground, in sports, and in life itself.

An even more vital task for us is to steer our children to the source of power when they feel inadequate for whatever they are facing. It's good to remember that the same wellspring of strength is available to us when we need it too. The morning of my first big speaking engagement, I woke up with a partial migraine, brought on, no doubt, by the stress and the untimely onset of "Aunt Mildred"—you know, menses. As I gripped the podium, my head ratcheted with pain, the words of a rather terrifying Slavic man rang through my consciousness. *"You can do it, Keri!"*

I did know I could do it, not because I was a sucker for punishment or a martyr, but for the simple reason that God would speak through me. He promised to be strong in my weakness, and weak I was. Floating on that prayer—and on some lovely pain meds—I gave my hour-long speech to hundreds of women in a packed auditorium. For me it was the equivalent of a double backflip on a sprained ankle. I was limp with relief—or maybe it was the meds!—and felt utterly triumphant. I could perform the daunting feat of speaking, coherently even, in front of this scary-big crowd because God said, "I can do it through you!"

I can do all things through Christ who strengthens me.

Philippians 4:13 NKJV

23: hold your horses

In [her] heart, a [wo]man plans [her] course,
but the LORD determines [her] steps.
Proverbs 16:9

When I worked in Christian publishing, the company I worked for published a book called *Ready, Set, Wait!* Inside the covers of this evocatively titled tome were stirring stories of God's people who waited on God through illness, job loss, infertility, and other hard, often agonizing circumstances. At the time, I thought about my sister-in-law, Lorraine, and her husband, Tracy, and their great desire to have a baby. Through their difficult struggle with infertility, I learned that men can be infertile just as often as women, though you never would know it. Guys are just much more uncomfortable chatting about their own physiology—go figure! A woman you've just met at a party will look you right in the eye and tell you about her episiotomy, but a man would rather miss the Super Bowl than share any such private details!

Tracy, however, was great, always brave and open about his struggles. As a family, we watched and prayed as Tracy submitted to all kinds of medical treatments and procedures, including daily hormone shots he injected himself. For years this couple prayed for a baby and visited specialist after specialist, who in turn ultimately gave them more bad news. Finally, they came to the end of the road, when an endocrinologist finally told them that medically there was nothing that could be done: there was no possible way for them to have a baby with Tracy's DNA.

Some ten years later, it seems as if God is still calling Tracy and Lorraine to wait. For a while it looked as if they were going to be led down the adoption road. A birth mother who knew Tracy's family picked them to raise her fourth baby. She had kept the first three, and all had different fathers. Her family lived in a trailer, and she worked to make ends meet as a night shelf stocker at Target. When this birth mother delivered a beautiful baby boy, it seemed as if Tracy and Lorraine's dreams were coming true at last. They named the baby Timothy John, which means "God is honored." When his birth mother changed her mind five days later and took Timmy back, it broke all our hearts. There is one photo of me, the proud aunt, beaming, holding Timmy. Whenever I see that photo, I get a lump in my throat as I remember all our dreams for that boy, our instant, profound attachment as his family—I so wanted to be his aunt!—and the pain that ensued when we knew we would never see him again. The picture also reminds me to pray for Timmy, now four years old.

As Tracy and Lorraine get older, the window of opportunity to be parents is slowly closing, and sometimes it's hard to understand God's purposes in their life. "Wait," God seems to be saying to them. "Wait for what I have for you." Like the Israelites in the desert for so long, this couple is cultivating a patience they never knew they could have. As they wait, God is active. Sometimes we have to cling to that bedrock truth.

Other loved ones of mine have had shorter waiting periods for a clear "yes!" My girlfriend Nancy, for example, waited about two years to be pregnant for the second time. After a year of trying, Nancy conceived, only to suffer an ectopic pregnancy.

The surgery ruptured her only viable fallopian tube, which made in vitro fertilization Nancy and her husband's only option. Expensive, invasive, and often frustrating, IVF can make the most patient of souls come unglued. Finally, after umpteen doctor's visits and her own hormone shots, Nancy became pregnant with twin boys, *big* boys, it appears, due to her husband's linebackerish, six-foot-eight stature. Be careful what you ask for, they always say! But of course, Nancy is thrilled. So am I, because I very much enjoy pregnancy in my friends—selecting baby gifts, loaning them tentlike maternity dresses, and passing out unsolicited advice! In Nancy's case, the waiting period ended, and now, when she delivers what may be sixteen pounds of baby, the fun will just be beginning.

At the moment, I am waiting for a child myself, a child who is growing, as I write these words, in her birth mother's womb on the other side of the world. Foreign adoption is a long, winding road full of setbacks and delays. And just when you think you have filled out your last scrap of paperwork, another couple of reams are thrown at you. Waiting to hold my baby daughter in my arms, to see her sweet face for the first time, is getting harder and harder. But I am holding on to the fact that God will sustain me and my family as we wait for Phoebe. And no matter how much I want to speed up the process, God is ordering my steps in his perfect time.

"I know the plans I have for you," declares the Lord,
"plans to prosper you, and not to harm you,
plans to give you hope and a future."

Jeremiah 29:11

24: tell your friend it's not a good time

A kindhearted woman gains respect.

Proverbs 11:16

It happens so often it's a wonder I'm not used to it by now. By "it" I mean the clanking of the door knocker, *clank, clank, clank,* followed by the persistent ringing of the doorbell, *ring, ring, ring.* Then more clanking, followed by pauses, and finally more ringing. These persistent efforts to be let into our house are made by Brightynn, a cute, blond, six-year-old girl who lives down the street. She has been put on this earth, partly, I sometimes think, to drive me around the bend—or at least to spur me on to greater levels of sanctification.

At first I thought she was adorable with her blue eyes, scruffy blond hair, and gap-toothed smiles. That was two years ago, when Brightynn and her family moved in a few doors down. All I knew was that pretty soon their then five-year-old was at our house every day, banging on the door, asking for snacks, often staying for dinner.

Brightynn was at our home probably at least forty times before I actually met one of her parents, who smelled like a distillery and seemed unclear about who we were. Of course, there was no way we were going to allow Jonah to play over at Brightynn's house, so the hospitality was 100 percent one-sided. Despite my efforts to consider her a ministry, I began to resent her constant presence in my house. She would pester the pets, tease Ez, barely more than a baby at the time, and hurt tender Jonah's feelings with her little mind games. (A favorite maneuver of hers was to flee out the door the second Jonah wanted to play something other than what she wanted to play. She could control the situation, she knew, and have complete dominance through this little manipulation.)

We also had to confront many unpleasant privacy issues when Brightynn was in our home. She would rummage around in our fridge with her grubby hands or burst through the bathroom door without knocking. One time I found her under my bedcovers playing hide-and-seek from Jonah.

"Boundaries," my friends told me. "You need to place some boundaries around this girl and her comings and goings."

I agreed. Brightynn was making me nuts, and I was at the point where I cringed at the sound of that clanking door. We told her she could no longer pull her little "If you don't play my game I'm leaving" stunt. Our bedroom was off-limits, and she had to ask for food nicely just as our kids had to. If she was allowed to stay for supper (no more than once or twice a week, we decided), she had to call her parents and ask for permission.

For the most part, Brightynn has complied with our rules. But the one thing she can't seem to compute is that, after a few tries knocking or ringing the doorbell, she should assume we are napping, in the shower, or I'm working in the basement, and to then go back home. Nope, naps are usually hit and miss, and I've lost count of how many times I've sat down at my computer rarin' to go, when the clanking started and wouldn't stop until I went and told her it wasn't a good time. *Sigh.* Sometimes all the feeling I can muster for that child is tolerance through gritted teeth.

So I pray for compassion, for love, for kindness. We want to open our home to her in Jesus's name, to be a haven for her from the instability, fear, and neglect she faces in her own home. On bad days only Christ's command to welcome a little one in his name makes me open that door with a smile pasted on my face and let Brightynn in, where she's sure to make a mess or cause a fight or intrude upon my privacy.

I heard once, from a wise Bible teacher, that God places difficult and unlovable people in our paths to expose some part of our souls that needs to grow and be challenged. This child certainly does that for me. Do you have a child—or adult—in your life who brings out the worst in you? May our heart's cry be that God continues to soften us, confront our selfishness, take us out of our comfort zones, and shape us into his image. May we always open the clanking doors in our lives and allow inside those whom he sends.

I tell you the truth, anyone who gives you a cup of cold water in my name . . . will certainly not lose his reward.
Mark 9:41

25: watch where you're going!

Watch your life and doctrine closely. . . .
Because if you do, you will save both
yourself and your hearers.

1 Timothy 4:16

I'm paranoid about stuff in my food. Whether I'm at a swanky restaurant or a fast-food drive-through, I especially examine my salad with great scrutiny. (By the way, if you're squeamish, you might want to skip this devotion. Or then again, you may want to be warned of what might happen to your salad! It's up to you.)

Why am I so nervous about eating salads prepared in restaurants? Well, it all started about four years ago when a friend of a friend saw a little green worm inch his merry way off the guy's date's plate and then scoot all the way across the table and over the edge like a barrel over Niagara Falls. The guy, not wanting to alarm his date (who would one day become his wife), didn't mention the little worm episode, figuring—typical man!—that no harm had been done. This couple appears to be happily wed despite the husband's dire mistake in not alerting his sweetie to the presence of a slithering worm on her food. I'm a girl, so I know this much: she would have wanted to know! Any female is going to want to know this information so that she can then lay down her fork and cease eating the recently vacated worm housing she thought was delicious, artfully arranged gourmet greens.

I myself ceased eating restaurant salads for two years, at which point I began rummaging through my salads with great zeal, leaving no leaf unturned. But sadly, lettuce is not the only type of food susceptible to unwanted items.

One time I found a twist tie in my soup. Of course, a twist tie is inanimate, which is a heap less disgusting than anything that crawls. But it was still unpleasant and not exactly appetizing. One of my kids could have choked on it, after all. So I said something about it to the waitress, and she explained that the bread bags lie on a shelf directly over the huge soup pot, thus the twist tie in my bowl.

Still, I haven't been nearly as vigilant with soups as I have been with salads. I figure the odds are excellent that I won't discover another nonfood item swimming in my soup, so why get suspicious? Besides, a twist tie is no worm.

But just as I began to think it was safe to dig into a bowl of greens without inspecting every veggie with a fine-toothed fork, I found a beetle in my salad. Yes, this time it was one of those truly marvelous new fast-food salads, a boon to every mom who doesn't want to gain quarter pounds every time she whips through the drive-through with the kiddies. The only reason I found the creepy, crawly culprit was that it started walking toward me. This little fellow was about the size of my pinkie fingernail, roughly the same hue as the spinach I was enjoying, with many legs and excellent locomotion. A sprightly wee thing, he might have been considered kind of cute had he not almost been crunched by my very own teeth. *Eewwwwww!*

Feeling kind of ill, I closed the lid of the salad, capturing the bug for evidence.

My husband—typical man!—was philosophical. "This can so easily happen with fresh produce," he waxed on. "Even if they wash the lettuce really well, a bug that color would be simple to miss." How many creepy crawlies have I missed in my lifetime despite my watchfulness? I don't want to know. The bigger question, though, is how often I miss more important things, metaphorical vermin, so to speak. The moral of this sad story is, it always pays to be alert, guarded, and observant, both in life and in salad.

Watch and pray so that you will not fall into temptation.

Matthew 26:41

26: what's going on in there?

You have set our iniquities before you,
our secret sins in the light of your presence.
Psalm 90:7

My fears came true one day when the phone rang. After the stunning conversation that followed, I realized my deepest inklings of doubt had been confirmed. The caller, motivated by a strong sense of divine nudging, revealed a secret to me that I never wanted to hear.

This brave Christian sister called to tell me that our babysitter, a twentysomething girl she was discipling, was covering up some scary things from me and the other day-care families. I hung up the phone and was overwhelmed with various emotions. Shock, that someone I trusted and genuinely cared for was duping me. Fear, for what might have happened had I not been told about her double life. Anger, that my precious child had possibly been in danger's way. All of these combustible feelings seethed in me, mingled with a sense of sadness that my friendship with our babysitter was about to come to a screeching halt.

Our babysitter, "Leona," had a love for children and a knack for making little people feel special. She had two children, one from a previous relationship and one from her marriage to "Esteban," a friendly young man who was going to college to complete his degree in social work. They attended our church, and when Leona opened the doors of her licensed in-home day-care center, several church families became her first customers.

Our son Jonah was two and a half when he started going to Leona's about three mornings a week. Her little house was immaculate, and she kept a tight ship with the kids. For the first time in his life, Jonah learned to take his plate to the dishwasher after he had finished eating. I was impressed with the home's atmosphere of fun, learning, and discipline. My social little man and the other kids at Leona's had a ball playing games and making projects.

I was delighted with this child-care arrangement, and I enjoyed getting to know Leona, as we would chat when I went to pick up Jonah. Over a few months, Leona's horrific story of past abuse and neglect unfolded in these conversations. I marveled at her resilience and ability to rise above a tragic childhood. Often Esteban would be home, playing with the kids in the yard. My heart was glad to see two young people with hard pasts forging ahead together to create new, redemptive lives.

Somehow, though, there was something amiss in that house. I couldn't put my finger on it, but my motherly instincts were alert to the possibilities. "You're being neurotic," I scolded myself. Apparently not.

According to the woman on the phone, Esteban was doing drugs as he had in the past, most likely not in front of the day-care kids, but he had definitely slid. Worse yet, Leona's brother Bobby, a cokehead, was drying out for a time in her basement. Jonah had mentioned "Uncle Bobby" hanging around, getting stuff out of the fridge, chatting with Leona. And Esteban had watched a pornographic movie one morning in front of one of the day-care kids. The child was just an infant, thank God, but it was clear that Esteban's boundaries were getting blurry fast. How soon would he slip up and do something inappropriate around one of the bigger kids, like mine?

When I told Leona that Jonah wouldn't be coming back to day care, she went nuts, as I suspected she would. She yelled and swore and even made veiled threats. I didn't even blame her. The woman felt incredibly threatened. Her whole livelihood was at stake. I truly felt awful. What would Leona do to make money for her family? The truth was she was an outstanding day-care provider, the best, most caring babysitter I could ask for. Yet there was no way Jonah was going back to that house.

When that secret came to light, everything changed for Leona and Esteban. Pastoral staff and lay leaders from church rushed in to do what they could to redeem the situation, but the damage had been done. Their marriage crumbled, and the scarred Mendoza family splintered again. Soon a For Sale sign was up in front of their little house, and the once pristine yard was thigh-high with overgrown grass.

I still have occasion to drive by that house. When I do, I have mostly sweet memories. I miss my bubbly, happy friend. I pray for Leona, Esteban, and their little girls, wherever they are. I think, *If those walls could talk . . .* Leona's house reminds me of the hurt and destruction secrets can wreak on people's lives and how God protected my child and others by whispering the truth into one faithful servant's spirit. It reminds me as well that my Father knows all and sees all, and that I should actively listen to him for guidance when it comes to my precious children.

Search me, O God, and know my heart.

Psalm 139:23

27: just a minute!

The fruit of the Spirit is . . . patience.

Galatians 5:22

Kids have little in the way of patience. If you're on the phone, they need something—*now*. If they want you to come play a game with them, they want you to come fifteen minutes ago. If the cutie patooties are hungry, they're *starving*. No matter how many times I've told my sons they aren't, in actual fact, starving, they seem to think they will expire in mere moments if not fed immediately.

"Just a minute!" If I had a nickel for every time I uttered those three words, I'd be in Palm Beach sipping a drink with an umbrella in it, killing time by the pool between spa treatments.

I find myself losing patience over the fact that my kids don't seem to have any to begin with. Waiting is not a favorite activity of my children, and come to think of it, I don't care much for it either. I have less than fond memories of waiting. Waiting, as a child, for my dad to come pick me and my brother and mom up for some doctor's appointment or something, bundled up to our eyebrows in winter outerwear, sweating buckets. Waiting in line for the bathroom at a concert and wishing for once

I could pass for a guy. Waiting for an important check to come after months of hard work. Arrgh! I'm such a product of our microwave society. I like things to proceed expediently, *clip-clop,* brisk, accelerated—you get the picture.

But before I became a mother, I actually fancied myself a patient person. After all, I didn't get irritated with tardy waitresses. *It's not their fault the food preparation is slow,* I would think. And rarely if ever would I honk my horn when Grandma Moses was tooling down the highway in front of me doing forty-five miles per hour in the left lane. *Let her have her fun now,* I'd muse, *because Sunset Manor is right around the corner for the old dear.*

And then I had a baby who grew into a cute but mulish toddler. Have you ever tried to rush a toddler? Toddlers have no concept that you have an agenda. They only know they would rather daydream, throw a fit, or refuse to budge than comply with your grown-up plans. When bustling around hurriedly with a toddler in the mix, sometimes the only option is picking the donkey up bodily and carting him like a sack of potatoes to wherever it is you want to go.

But you know this already, because you live it every day! Patience can run quite thin on both sides of the mom/kid equation. It's just not a virtue that comes naturally to most people, if the people I've met have been any indication.

Yet the Bible seems to be quite big on patience, mentioning it dozens of times as a quality to be admired and cultivated. I think the divine definition of patience, though, contains a far deeper meaning than simply not honking your horn at geezers on the road. Built into this desired fruit is trust, endurance, courage, and calmness. It's believing that God is at work, even if by all outward appearances a situation seems to have ground to a screeching halt. It's bravery in the face of futility, and peace instead of panic.

When Doyle and I were newlyweds, we faced a very unexpected bout of unemployment, financial crises, and even a semblance of homelessness. At one point we were living in one of those rent-by-the-week motels, two thousand miles from home in a soggy coastal town in Washington. Our resumes, such as they were from two green college graduates, were turned down time and again, and there seemed to be no light at the end of the tunnel. For three months we lived off of wedding money, pounding the pavement and getting more downtrodden by the day. Our beautiful wedding presents, crystal, china, and silverware sat in boxes in our new/old rusty tank of a truck. Their very presence mocked our bare-bones existence.

During those trying weeks and months, I came across the plight of the prophet Habakkuk, and his predicament seemed strikingly similar to my own. Despite his prayers and longing for freedom from the Babylonians and grinding poverty, Habakkuk and the people of Israel had waited what seemed like eons for the circumstances to change. But in the midst of God's seeming inactivity, Habakkuk endured and even rejoiced: "Though the fig tree does not bud and there are no grapes on the vines . . . yet I will rejoice in the LORD, I will be joyful in God my Savior" (Hab. 3:17–18). Those words sustained me and helped me develop patience against the day that my own figurative "fig tree" grew buds. Within a few months, Doyle and I both had jobs—not great jobs, but after all that waiting and hoping, they were enough. It taught me that God is always worthy of trust and patience, even when circumstances seem hopeless.

And so after waiting patiently,
Abraham received what was promised.

Hebrews 6:15

28: what's that smell?

Let my prayer be counted as incense before thee,
and the lifting up of my hands
as an evening sacrifice.

Psalm 141:2 (RSV)

My husband thinks I have turbo-charged olfactory glands. It never fails to boggle his mind how I can smell things before he can—if he ever does! "What's that smell?" I'll ask suspiciously, sniffing the air for more scented evidence.

"What smell? What are you talking about?" he'll say, looking at me like I'm a bit loopy.

"I think it's the baby," I'll say, sighing with the knowledge that this means someone is getting up to deal with a diaper detonation.

"No way! I just changed him, what? Like five minutes ago!" My husband will look shocked and filled with indignation that our son could unload in his pants so soon after being swabbed and changed. "Still, I don't smell anything. I think you're imagining things."

But you know how babies are. They aren't at all concerned with the timing of their bodily extrusions. And usually, when

Mom thinks something may be rotten in Denmark, she's right. We parents need keen senses of smell to detect various things that need immediate detecting. Like a dirty diaper, of course, or spit-up (it's good to get that out of your hair before you leave the house in the morning), or maybe a pet's accident. No one wants to be surprised with a shoe full of that!

Thankfully, there's a flip side for my sharp sense of smell. We have so many fabulous aromas to enjoy on this earth. Fresh roasted Costa Rican coffee. Artisanal bread baking. Peonies in June.

And experts say smell can stir our memories like no other sense. When I was a college student in downtown Chicago, there was a chocolate factory near the campus, and once in a while the aroma of chocolate would waft around me, tantalizing, torturing, until I couldn't stand another second without a bag of M&M's. Now the perfume of melting chocolate takes me back to college every single time.

Doyle's parents recently remodeled their farmhouse, which is a positive thing in every aspect except for one detail: the new construction mandated that they tear down the breezeway to the house. I loved to walk into that house and linger in the breezeway for a few extra seconds just so I could inhale the beloved, never-forgotten smell of my grandma's entranceway. Grandma's house was also situated on a farm, though hers was set on hundreds of acres of wheat and canola and flax, and Doyle's parents' place is nestled in forty acres of woods and hay fields.

Both country abodes shared a similar scent. The fragrance, almost indefinable as many aromas are, was a bouquet of old wood, loamy earth, apples, and melted snow. It wasn't necessarily a pleasurable smell, like something a candle maker would infuse into hand-dipped wax. If the smell were in a candle, it would probably be named something like "Fruit Cellar/Old Barn/Muddy Boots," nothing most folks would care to burn in their homes. But that scent to me was beautiful and fragrant like no other. Why? Because breathing it in brought back, just for a few seconds, my cherished grandma.

I could almost imagine her coming to the door, a smile on her face, soon to enfold me in a warm hug. She really was a storybook grandma, with a bun in her hair, an ample bosom, and old-fashioned aprons. And in my in-law's breezeway, just for a moment, I would be transported to McTavish, Manitoba, the pin dot town where my grandma's little house on the prairie stands.

In that house, delectable roast beef was cooked, the Low German dialect was spoken, and love was doled out freely and without reserve. For me "Fruit Cellar/Old Barn/Muddy Boots" is aromatherapy at its finest.

Devotional writer Louise Bergmann DuMont writes, "God is not immune to the blessing of an aromatic scent. When we pray according to his will, he receives our words as fragrant incense floating up to heaven for his pleasure."[6]

Sometimes the scent is less than pleasurable. God can detect when my attitude is sour, my motives impure, my thoughts tainted with self instead of soul. Yet he, like my beautiful grandma, holds his arms open to embrace his child. Let's pray that our prayers and offerings are sweet to him, always.

They are a fragrant offering . . . pleasing to God.

Philippians 4:18

29: just wait 'til your father comes home

No eye has seen, no ear has heard,
no mind has conceived what God has prepared
for those who love him.

1 Corinthians 2:9

Jonah has a framed sampler on his wall of a choo-choo train. It's quite small, maybe six inches by six inches and is really out of place in a macho six-year-old's den. The thing has fallen off the wall a bunch of times, and I sometimes think it might be time to put it away. But how do you put away such a treasure? You see, the sampler was stitched with love by my childhood best friend, Lori, who made it for Jonah right after he was born. My beautiful friend with the sweet spirit and infectious laugh died not long afterward, finally losing her long and valiant battle with cancer after thirteen years. The choo-choo train is one of the few things I have of hers, and I will cherish it always, along with her class ring and the sweatshirt she got when she and her husband won a trip to Wimbledon in the last year of her life.

It has been poignant for me to watch my son Jonah's friendship with his classmate Ethan unfold, because it reminds me of Lori and me. "It's rare that two kindergartners would have such a close friendship," Jonah's teacher told me. I'm glad that my son seems to have inherited my need for friends and that he found such a great buddy during his first year of school. When Lori and I met, it too was in kindergarten. We had a mean teacher, one of those nasty people who has no business sullying the educator's noble profession. Anyway, Ms. Meanie (I've blocked out her actual name) had scolded me for not being able to tie my hat and had commanded me to stay after school until the hat was tied. Flustered, with my sensitive soul bruised, I fumbled with the hat strings to no avail. But then Lori McCaskill, a quiet, tall girl who lived on my street, snuck behind Ms. Meanie's back to where I was struggling to maintain my dignity and tied my hat for me. We left together, hand in hand, new amigos who would share the bonds of friendship for twenty-six years until her death.

The last year of Lori's life, the Lord began to bring memories to her mind of various exposures she had to him through our friendship—snippets of conversations she and I had about God, the Bible, and salvation; pieces of Bible stories she heard while attending our family's basement Bible club; remnants of my clumsy attempts to witness to her. These things that she recalled rolled back the years to when we were little girls. I barely even remembered she had attended our little Bible club, never mind actual quotes from those bygone days. But the Holy Spirit quickened long-buried memories and made them stand out in Lori's consciousness.

That same year, God placed her on my heart and mind relentlessly. Before we even knew she was terminally ill, God put notions in my head to phone her, to pray for her, to plan a dinner with her on my next trip home. Her interest in spiritual things and my interest in her dovetailed perfectly, and many precious conversations took place between the two of us old friends. Those seeds planted long ago in childhood came to bear wonderful, abundant fruit as Lori accepted Jesus as her Savior about three months before her death.

Lori's funeral was both incredibly difficult and amazingly miraculous. I grieved her terribly, and during my tribute to Lori that day, I was so overcome I thought my knees would give way. But it was also a blessed event, with no fewer than four hundred folks, mostly unchurched, hearing the gospel message of hope and redemption. We probably won't know until heaven what transpired in the hearts of those who came to pay their final respects to this kind and friendly young woman. I also won't know, exactly, why God chose to take Lori then, at age thirty-one, leaving behind a husband and parents and friends who needed her so much. "Why did God take my angel?" Lori's mom sobbed to me one morning over their kitchen table. Maybe one reason is because both Lori's parents came to know Jesus soon after she died. Maybe, because I just don't know for sure. But my Father knows, and I'm going to ask him when he takes me home.

He will wipe every tear from their eyes.
There will be no more death or mourning or crying or pain,
for the old order of things has passed away.

Revelation 21:4

30: turn down that music

Let them praise his name with dancing and
make music to him with tambourine and harp.

Psalm 149:3

Our family might be tooling along in the minivan, rocking out to some tunes on the radio or CD player, when suddenly a thought hits Doyle and me, and we look at each other in amazement: this slice of family life is completely different than anything that transpired during our own childhoods! When we were Jonah and Ezra's age, our parents would have no sooner played rock 'n' roll in the old paneled station wagons than they would have tattooed peace symbols on their foreheads. My parents were strictly old school. Often the radio at our house would have German hymns coming out of it. Even polka music would have been a jolly improvement, but polka was a little too connected to the beer tent crowd for my folks' taste. The only "secular" things coming out of the family radio were broadcasts of Winnipeg Jets games.

My personal album collection was highlighted by Little Marcy screeching "Jesus Wants Me for a Sunbeam" in a tone so high-pitched surely the dogs down the block could pick up on it. If my parents had known then that someday I would write extensively about rock music, they probably would have driven that Mercury Montego station wagon straight into a prairie ditch from the sheer shock of it.

Thankfully, right around the time I was about to enter junior high, the oldsters lightened up. In fact, my dad, a Christian bookseller, threw his support solidly behind the Christian rock scene and brought home all kinds of Christian albums. Wisely, he didn't get tied up in knots about the number of beats per minute or the fact that drums may have originated in pagan African rituals. Some of my friends' parents were very legalistic about the sound of the music. If it was too "heavy" or "hard," they reasoned, it must be straight from the pit. I am so grateful my dad went way out of his comfort zone to steer his young teen daughter to rock music that praised God. Hence my teen years were spent rocking out to Amy Grant, Whiteheart, and even heavy metal bands such as Jerusalem and Stryper (yes, Stryper, with the spandex and makeup. Those guys were prettier than me!). If the lyrics were edifying enough to be sold in his store, they were pure enough to be listened to at high volume in his daughter's bedroom.

"Worldly" music though was a different story. My dad and I had many tussles over that issue. He was a big connoisseur of those "Why Knock Rock?" books that came out in the eighties, the ones in which you could look up just about any particular band or artist and have every sin they ever committed listed in alphabetical order. So it took me, oh, a decade or so before I could select mainstream music without having some hang-ups about it.

On balance, though, my dad did pave the way for me to become a huge fan of rock music, and now I love it that my kids can jam and worship God at the same time. Just as my dad gave me the gift of music in my cultural vernacular, so I want my guys to feel abundantly free to rock out to the glory of God. We want to teach our sons to vet their tunes—Christian or not—through the grid of a Jesus-centered worldview so they can make good choices in the powerful arena of music.

Like Amy Grant once said, "Music moves you in a direction before you even know you're headed there." Songs can lift your spirit, give voice to your deepest emotions, and point you to the maker of all music. I'm so glad the Scriptures, especially the Psalms, extol the Lord through instruments, music, and dance. What that teaches me is that we are to enjoy, revel in, thrill to, and bless all kinds of music. Whether you'd rather listen to the Fugees than a fugue, or you'd choose a bossa nova over a blues bass line, music is a beautiful, wondrous gift. Celebrate that gift often and well!

Praise him with the clash of cymbals,
praise him with resounding cymbals.
Let everything that has breath praise the Lord.

Psalm 150:5–6

31: don't get too big for your britches

Blessed are the meek.

Matthew 5:5

There's nothing like a couple of kids to keep you eating humble pie. It's hard to be stuck-up about much when you're changing diapers, tripping on toys, and coming up empty on answers to everything from why the sky is blue and not red to when God was born.

"But, Mom, God hadda been borned sometime!"

"Well, actually, God is the only one who was never born. He just always was here."

"So how old is God if he never been borned?"

"Umm . . . He's super-duper, awesomely old, okay?" Of course, this answer is not okay, and round and round we go. It never ceases to amaze me the way my kids make me feel like I might not be the sharpest tool in the shed.

Take Bionicles, those vaguely Darth Vaderish–looking warriors that boys like to assemble out of a zillion Lego pieces. Jonah got one for his fifth birthday, and as soon as we got that thing home, he was begging for me to put it together. You must understand I am almost completely right-brained. The left lobes where math and mechanics should be located are pretty much devoid of functioning cells.

Since I wanted to please my son, I took a deep breath, unfolded the instructions, and laid the multitude of small pieces in front of me. Forehead burrowed, eyes narrowed, lips pursed in concentration, I painstakingly built a rather spiffy, scary-looking fellow in about forty-five minutes. Pleased, I presented the Gali Nouva to my son, who instantly ascertained my error.

"Mom, he looks weird!"

Then my five-year-old took his Bionicle apart and reassembled him, correctly, in about twenty minutes. So much for being the savvy, know-it-all grown-up!

My friends who have older kids tell me that that feeling of knowing very little just gets worse as children reach their preteen and teen years. Author and counselor Dan Allender tells the story of how his thirteen-year-old once confounded him with a wise-beyond-her-years moment. One Thanksgiving, Allender says, Amy asked if she could possibly not go to the family feast that year.

"No way," was his response. "But why do you ask?"

She said she was tired of her dad and other assorted male relatives gorging themselves on the holiday bounty, then plopping in front of the Big Game until it was time for pie. "I'd rather go to a soup kitchen this year," Amy said, "and help serve people who have no food." Allender was flabbergasted, completely leveled by his daughter's insight into human nature and the way she nailed his rather decadent attitude toward the Thanksgiving feast.

Humbled? Dad was as meek as a lamb at that moment. His feeling was even more ignoble than mine when I failed to construct a toy designed for elementary school–aged children. Why? Because Allender's daughter had exposed a weak spot in her father's character. *Ouch*. You can bet, though, that Amy's dad never viewed the pass-the-pie-and-pass-out ritual the same way again.

God knows our kids can bring us down to size maybe better than anyone else. In the warp and woof of daily life together, they see their moms and dads exactly as we are, warts and all. It's easy to put up a façade of togetherness before friends and acquaintances but much harder to fake it around the children God has given us to raise.

Our Father uses our kids to bring us down a notch or two, preferably to our knees, where we have no choice but to seek divine insight, wisdom, and courage. That's where God wants us, softhearted, pliable, open to his instruction and guidance. We may think we can complete our work, maintain our closest relationships, and fulfill our calling as parents on our own. Clearly, though, we can't—we have our kids to give us timely reminders of that!—and the sooner we learn that the smoother our journeys will be.

Humble yourself in the sight of the Lord,
and He will lift you up.
James 4:10 NKJV

32: don't tease the dog

As servants of God we commend ourselves
in every way . . . in understanding,
patience, and kindness.

2 Corinthians 6:4, 6

Sometimes it's all I can do to be nice to the dog. Now you canine devotees out there are all bent out of shape, but let me just say I'm a huge fan of other people's dogs. And I blubber with the best of them at three-hankie movies featuring a brave/sad/dying dog. I sobbed myself silly during *Old Yeller* ("Best doggone dog in the West . . ."). But you haven't met Dinah. It's true that I am a cat person. Since I was thirteen and got a kitten named Toby, I've been all about the felines and their slinky selves. For nine years, Doyle and I had Pierre, who was actually one of the meanest cats I've ever encountered (he sent the mailman to an urgent care center from scratching him through the mail slot), but my love for cats persevered.

Cats are lighter than dogs. They can't knock you over when you're a wobbly toddler, and they make no noise when they are padding around the house. Once in a while, they meow to say

"Howdy," or "Feed me," or "Let me out of the house, as there appears to be a bird I would like to chase." Cats purr. Cats slink. Cats pad. They luxuriate in the sunshine and oh-so-delicately wash their little paws. One thing I adore about cats is their lack of smell. Rarely do I catch a whiff of anything unpleasant on Talullah, our new gray barn cat, which is infinitely more than I can say about that stinky mutt of a dog we happen to own. Doyle actually likes Dinah's smell. Eau de Hound Dog, he says, evokes all kinds of pleasant thoughts about hunting and farms and wide-open front porches. Dinah Blue smells like *Where the Red Fern Grows*, if it were a scratch and sniff book, Doyle has opined more than once.

I think that on this issue my dear husband is off his rocker. The dog just stinks. She also sheds like no other beast I've ever encountered in my life, coating our clothes, furniture, and floors with a layer of white hair. I could knit a sweater with all that hair. Additionally, that dog of ours could win a gold medal in barking at squirrels. Half my life is spent shushing her, sweeping up after her, or tripping over her.

Why don't we just get rid of her, you may well wonder, if she's such a royal pain in the hindquarters? Doyle loves her. He talks baby talk to her the minute he walks in the door from work. "Ohhhh, there's my stinky old hound dog," he'll croon three inches from her snout while scratching her ears. It's enough to make you sick, that's what.

Ezra also bears great affection for the pooch, snuggling up to her while watching a movie or talking to her while he's playing outside. What kind of mom would get rid of a beloved family pet, even though that pet can be excruciatingly annoying? Hey, I may not like her, but I'm not Cruella deVille.

It's no use. She's with us for the duration, come what may. I have a feeling Dinah will live to be a ripe old grande dame of basset hounds, and that means I have to tolerate the smell, the hair, and the barking for at least another decade. *Sigh*.

But it just may be that my less-than-beloved pet is working undercover as an agent of my sanctification. Follow me on this: we have always taught our kids to be kind to animals. From the time they could crawl and clutch a handful of kitty or doggy hair, we have drilled into them the importance of being gentle with pets. Why? Because it's really a core value of life to be kind to those who are weaker than us. I'm no animal rights activist, although I am an animal lover, Dinah notwithstanding. And Jesus didn't die for animals and trees, he died for people. But I truly do believe that how we treat animals is a mark of our character. When that pea-brained fleabag is pushing every button I have, I think back to the words of a devotional I had as a teenager: "The very cat or dog in your house should benefit from your being a Christian." Dinah Blue will bark to that!

The fruit of the spirit is . . . kindness.

Galatians 5:22

33: mommy will kiss your boo-boo and make it all better

He heals the brokenhearted and
binds up their wounds.

Psalm 147:3

In the good old summertime, I always keep a stash of Band-Aids, antiseptic spray, and antibacterial ointment right by the back door in case of boo-boos. Then when knees are scraped, elbows dinged, and other body parts bitten by bugs, mom can make like Florence Nightingale and nurse the victim back to health. Ever notice how Band-Aids disappear faster than Popsicles on a hot July day? That's because kids love the novelty and special, important feeling of wearing a Band-Aid. Double the vanishing rate when the bandages sport a motif of some sort, say SpongeBob SquarePants or Clifford the Big Red Dog. Then you can count on multiple "wounds" per day.

We've recently instituted a "no blood, no bandage" rule, which seems to work pretty well in saving Band-Aids. (It's actually pretty funny to see the boys get such a thrill out of a speck of blood or the teeniest scrape, because those mean they get to wear Scooby Doo on their foot for two hours! Woo-hoo!) But what does a savvy mom do when her bellowing offspring has a legitimate hurt, but there's no blood?

One of the boys' babysitters is a competent woman named Dawn who has five children and who could manage a few more with one hand tied behind her back. Do you know the type of woman I'm talking about? She has all kinds of tricks up her sleeve to deal with the never-ending slew of crises and situations that arise with young kids.

One of my favorites is her "ice pack" MO. When one of Dawn's children or charges is afflicted with something like a bruised knee or a whacked funny bone, she gets out a package of frozen veggies and has the child apply it to the injury until such time as the victim feels duly healed. This is a brilliant way to help kids cope with the many boo-boos they get in the rough and tumble of life. Not only does a bag of okra bring down the swelling of a banged-up ankle, but it also provides lots of validation for the little one's bruised psyche. It gives the message that Mommy or Miss Dawn cares so much about their ouchie that she is giving them an ice pack to make the pain go away. *I must be special,* they think, clutching their frozen panacea to their sore spot, *if I merit such serious treatment.*

This method works especially well for injuries that are more emotional than physical. Oh, the child may have twisted his leg a wee bit in his wrestling match with his brother, but mainly his ego was battered by the fact that he didn't come out on top. An "ice pack" is attention, authentication, and TLC all wrapped up in one frosty sack of lima beans. And after about five minutes of ice-cold therapy, the injured one is ready to relinquish the ice pack back to the freezer and move on. I find it cuts down on protracted crying and complaining about getting hurt too. Once the ice pack is applied, tears usually dry up fast.

If only our little hurts could be healed as easily as our kids'. When a friend's words give us the emotional equivalent of a paper cut, we sting inside. When our husbands seem to take us for granted, our hearts are bruised. And when a fellow church member doesn't appear to value our contributions, our spirits bear the markings of a welt.

Thankfully, though we aren't kids anymore, we are the daughters of a tender and loving Father who promises to bind up our wounds, big and small. Just as we willingly kiss our children's scrapes and bruises, so God gently scoops us up in his strong arms and comforts, consoles, and heals our hurting spirits.

How gracious God will be when you cry for help!
As soon as he hears, he will answer you.

Isaiah 30:19

34: no, you can't change your name

A good name is more desirable
than great riches.

Proverbs 22:1

I'm a name freak. I love helping my friends, acquaintances—strangers off the street!—come up with suitable monikers for their babies. My first book was a guide to baby names from the Bible, and those months spent researching names and their histories and meanings were among the most enjoyable of my writing career.

When someone tells me he or she was assisted in bestowing a handle on their offspring through one of my books or articles, I am truly humbled. Naming someone is a deeply personal process, and it binds namer and namee forever. To know there are little tykes running around this planet answering to Chloe, Silas, Boaz (yes, Boaz!), Adam, Benjamin, Josiah, and many other names, in some small measure because of my enthusiasm for names, is thrilling.

Naming a child is a multifaceted endeavor. A parent must hash through meanings, sounds, evocations, and popularity of names. Does the fact that a name has a profoundly spiritual meaning, such as "gift of God," or "Jehovah has heard" edge it onto the contenders' list? Or will a banal meaning such as "to dig" or "dusty ditch" be just fine? Is the sound of the name euphonious and pleasing, and does it go with a last name? What does the name, when said aloud, bring to people's minds? Numerous studies have been done on the effects of a name's "image." For example, my friend's daughter, Zion Esther (sister to Boaz Kazimier, by the way!), will have vastly different expectations in her lifetime than a classmate given the much more subdued identity of Taylor Marie. People with rather unwieldy monikers such as Bertha or Hilda have been shown to struggle somewhat in school and in their careers, as opposed to their classmates with more attractive names.

Many parents, obviously, are comfortable with the fact that their child will share his or her name with any number of friends, teammates, and colleagues when they pluck a hugely popular name such as Emily or Jacob off the top of the chart. Others, like the mothers of Fracaswell and Praxilla—real names, incidentally—are boldly going where no baby namers have gone before (and where no baby namers should ever go again?).

Other factors get thrown into the mix as well. Do you want to honor a relative by dusting off the old cedar chest and reviving Mabel or Bertrand? Will Grandma Irmgard be offended if you bypass her clunky handle for something prettier (which would be almost anything, but don't tell her that). Ethnicity is another component of the process. If you are Puerto Rican and your husband is Irish, do you lean toward Delimar and Marisol or toward Fiona and Aisling? Perhaps God ordained our pregnancies to last nine months so we would have time to evaluate all these factors before making our decision!

We found Jonah and Ezra in the Old Testament, obviously. We loved their ancient roots, spiritual reverberations, and modern sensibilities. I am fascinated by the way my sons have lived into their names. Hopefully they won't want to change them, at least in my lifetime. I think that may be more of a girl thing anyway. Two cousins of mine, dubbed Dorothy and Margaret by their mother (who had nine children to name), legally changed their names to Rietta (a piece of her middle name, Henrietta) and Margeaux. I suspect this broke their mother's heart. Naming a child is so personal, so meaningful, that changing one's name seems like an insult.

I've always thought Adam was fortunate to get the chance to name the animals and birds. I'm going to ask God someday why he didn't just name them himself. (I notice the Creator did name some of his handiwork: "He determines the number of stars," Psalm 147:4 says, "and calls them each by name.")

Our Father in heaven also calls us by name. We are the crowning glory of his creation, and when he whispers to us in our spirits, we are as precious to him as if we were only children. As much thought and effort we put into naming our beloved children, our Father invests infinitely more into engraving our names in the Book of Life.

But rejoice that your names are written in heaven.

Luke 10:20

35: be nice to your sister

Clothe yourselves with compassion.

Colossians 3:12

My friend and I were talking in the doorway of her home after I dropped off her kids. We were chitchatting about the weather, an upcoming trip to Illinois, her child's recent hospital visit, school, homework, grades—you name it. There was nothing in her demeanor that suggested she was anything but a happy young mother juggling with good grace the endless assortment of duties that come with parenthood.

I was about to take off when her face suddenly crumpled. Normally strong and upbeat, "Marjo" was struggling to keep it all together. "Are you okay?" I asked, even though the answer was obvious.

"It's just my marriage," she explained, brokenly, obviously trying to regain her composure before her kids or mine reentered the room. "I just don't know how I'm going to keep this thing going. He's . . . He's . . . He's just so *cold,*" she said, swiping tears from her face with the back of her hand.

I was both shocked and not shocked. I knew Marjo's husband to be a difficult man, rather full of himself and unyielding. But then again, I always thought that somehow the two of them meshed, that her sweet, phlegmatic personality complemented his take-charge, bullish ways. But one never really knows what goes on in other people's marriages.

"Oh, Marjo," I said, "I'm so sorry." I knew there was nothing I could do to help her, really, other than listen with empathy. We talked about their efforts with a marriage counselor, how even though her husband would hear the counselor, he fundamentally refused to make changes in his dealings with Marjo. Nevertheless, counseling had given Marjo the tools to confront his behavior and ask for what she needed in the marriage. Unfortunately, the man she married wasn't interested in what she needed. It was his way or the highway, basically.

Knowing Marjo's bedrock decency and goodness, I immediately felt defensive on her behalf. It takes two to tango, as they say, but I knew she held little of the blame for the deterioration of her union. I hugged her and promised to pray, hoping my listening ear had given her a small measure of comfort. "I just want to keep this marriage going until my kids are gone," she said sniffling.

My heart sank as I reflected on the situation, which seemed bleak. It would take a miracle for Marjo's unyielding husband to soften his stance. Their whole family was at risk of dissolving in divorce court. Of course, God could penetrate the coldest heart and turn Marjo and her husband toward each other again. I prayed that he would, because I felt very sorry for my friend that day. Her sorrow had pierced my heart.

Her situation reminded me of other stories related over the years by friends who were hurting in their marriages. Weeks before Marjo's confession, a tearful friend in another state had revealed her stunning sense of betrayal: she had discovered her husband's illicit activities on the Internet—pornography and chat room flirtations. It wasn't the first time, sadly, I'd heard that particular grievance, but that didn't make it any less painful to hear.

Whenever one of my friends is beaten down by something, a rough patch in her marriage, the sickness or death of a loved one, difficulties with children, unemployment . . . my heart is heavy. I always vow to pray for them, and I do, but there's always room for improvement. As Christians, we have a mandate to go beyond pity and truly bear each other's burdens. Sometimes tea and sympathy are enough and act as a soothing balm for a troubled spirit. At other times, Christlike compassion requires rolling up our sleeves and putting our money, time, and efforts where our mouths are. For me, this could mean babysitting for Marjo to give her some space to think and pray, or just not forgetting her plight in my busyness and consistently petitioning God—Father to us both—on her behalf.

I don't know where I would be if I hadn't had my friends, my sisters, to lift me up, cheer me on, and never let me give up hope. Let's ask God for a heart that is others oriented, soft toward the hurting, and strong enough to shoulder a sister who has been weakened by a heavy load.

Carry each other's burdens,
and in this way you will fulfill the law of Christ.

Galatians 6:2

36: mommy's on the treadmill

Do you not know that your body is a temple of the Holy Spirit, who is in you, whom you have received from God?

1 Corinthians 6:19

I'm a big fitness buff. Yes, it's true. I love nothing more than to hop on the old elliptical machine for forty-five minutes, huffing and puffing, once or twice a week, whether I need it or not. Of course, I'm usually reading *USA Today* and maybe watching TV at the same time. It's dubious if I'm getting my heart rate up high enough to put a dent in my thighs, but at least I've pretty much been holding steady weightwise. In my case, "steady" means I haven't really gained weight but I haven't really lost weight either—that's since Baby Ezra came three years and three months ago, but who's counting?

Sigh. Since becoming a mom, keeping fit has been one whale of a challenge. (Since I had a baby named Jonah, the whole whale theme rings all too true!) Debra Waterhouse, who wrote the fantastic book *Outsmarting the Female Fat Cell after Pregnancy*, says that postpartum our bodies change the way we deal with fat. Months and even years after giving birth, our physiques fight to keep fat stored in our thighs and tummies just in case our babies might need that fat in the form of nutrition. We are much more resistant, she says, to burning fat than before we became mothers.

This means for most of us (not counting our oh-so-svelte cousins and girlfriends who bounce right back into their prebaby jeans) that health and fitness become an uphill climb after we bring home our first bundle of joy.

None of us would trade her cherubs to wake up and be a size 6. We would readily agree that our little ones are worth every dimple, pouch, and purple zigzag that giving birth to them incurred. Nonetheless, it's discouraging to try harder and achieve fewer results. Maybe this sense of discouragement is why young mothers suffer from more eating disorders than any other demographic group. It's true. One might think that as grown-ups and parents, moms would have it all together in the body image department, but studies show that even teenagers don't suffer from the same angst about their shapes as young moms do.

Waterhouse says that 96 percent of women harbor some sense of dissatisfaction about their bodies, which means the vast majority of us are *disordered* eaters even if we don't have true eating disorders.

Our culture of thin certainly doesn't help. We see star moms like Cindy Crawford and Sarah Jessica Parker return within weeks to their beautiful, lean shapes, and we feel pressure to look like them. We know those ladies have personal trainers and probably personal chefs to put them through their paces, but we still feel, however subtly, somewhat burdened to be a red-hot mama just like them. On television, moms are fabulous and fit, despite their sitcom pregnancies that featured massive donut cravings and whatnot.

The message gets through: even moms are supposed to look hot. Adding insult to injury, our bodies fight us every step of the way, and we end up discouraged and even depressed. What I try to focus on is this: God wants me to be healthy, to glorify him with my eating and exercise habits. It's easy to take our cues from popular culture and buy into the constant newsflash that there is no such thing as too thin. As Christian women, we need to be countercultural, to care more about what God wants us to look like than trying to look like Jennifer Aniston. He is the only one who can truly help us become disciplined about our bodies. He is also the only one who can fill that void inside that we sometimes try to fill with a bag of Oreos. Our Father wants us to turn to him when we feel down about our bodies. He wants to do an extreme makeover in our hearts, surgically removing false ideals, insecurities, and preoccupations. Next time we feel sad that our fat jeans have become our everyday jeans, let's invite the best personal trainer in the galaxy in on our self-talk about body image. When we take our struggles and issues to him in prayer, he will be faithful to come alongside us and reshape us, inside and out.

For we are God's workmanship.

Ephesians 2:10

37: i'll love you forever

Train a child in the way he should go, and when he is old he will not turn from it.

Proverbs 22:6

The funny thing about kids is that they aren't one-size-fits-all. Even a couple of confreres like Jonah and Ezra, who look so much alike that we joke they are twins three years apart, have major differences wired into their personality hard drives. Jonah is more sensitive, hates being kissed, thinks girls have cooties, and counts among his personal interests hockey and sharks. Ezra is in your face, which is sometimes good and sometimes not so good. He adores kisses and loves to snuggle on the couch while watching a movie or reading a book. But cross him and watch out! Ez will respond with so much fury and angst you expect to see smoke coming out of his ears. So far he thinks girls are swell, especially girls who like horses. He couldn't be bothered with slap shots or how many teeth a shark has, but he talks incessantly about Grandpa's four horses and is mesmerized by anything horse-related.

Yup, they're different animals, my two sons, so I try to work with them differently to achieve the same kinds of behavior goals. They also give and receive love in distinct ways.

Experts, like author Gary Smalley, talk about the five love languages that each person on the planet has. We all have a primary love language, he says, and maybe one or two secondary love languages. To follow Smalley's theory, we feel loved—or not—based on whether or not our parents, spouse, siblings, and friends speak our love language to us. Mine is gifts, that much I know. I not only love to receive gifts, but I anticipate most all holidays—Christmas, Easter, Valentine's Day, St. Patrick's Day, and so on—with glee because they are opportunities to hand out gifts as well. People with the gift love language don't require expensive presents (although a pricey token of esteem certainly wouldn't be turned down). Even one's favorite candy bar or a solitary bloom plucked from a flower bucket is enough to make the gift person feel loved.

Jonah's secondary love language is gifts. No matter where I'm going, when I get home he always says, "What'd you bring me, Mom?" I used to think he was greedy, until I realized he just wants to know I've been thinking about him. Jonah's primary love language is undeniably quality time. If I spend just half an hour playing Go Fish with him or shooting a plastic puck around the deck, he is noticeably happier and easier to get along with.

Ezra operates on a whole other axis. He feels loved and cared for when we hug him and kiss him and hold him on our laps. When he was just learning to walk, he would toddle over to me for a "love fix" a few times a day; just a quick squeeze and he was recharged, ready to explore his universe again. His primary love language is definitely touch.

Doyle? Well, I have a sneaking suspicion his love language might be acts of service. You know—clean laundry, dinner on the table, his clothes picked out for him by the local fashion policewoman. When it dawned on me that acts of service might be my husband's main way of feeling loved, my response was "Uh-oh." I'm the furthest thing from a domestic diva there ever was. The only housework I like doing are things related to decorating. I pick out a mean bathroom fixture, and our new denim slipcovers look fetching if I do say so myself. Oh, and I throw a very nice birthday party for the boys too. But baking a cake in the shape of a horse's head once a year doesn't count for much on the domestic front. Cooking? Cleaning? Ironing? I repeat: "Uh-oh."

What I've discovered, to my profound relief, is that Doyle doesn't need me to iron the tablecloth or his boxers (thank goodness for that!), nor does he require a home-cooked meal on the table at 6:00 sharp every night. He is actually very equitable about sharing the housework/childcare load. But my wonderful guy truly does appreciate it when I do dig around the clean socks pile (otherwise known as "The Quagmire") and come up with a matching pair of work socks for him. It's a small thing, but putting together a pair of socks for the man makes him feel cared for.

We all need different things to make us feel loved. When we love our kids and spouses in the way they need to be loved, experts say, they won't look for the false love the world offers. That challenges me and motivates me every day.

I feel glad knowing God speaks my love language perfectly every day.

He will take great delight in you,
he will quiet you with his love.

Zephaniah 3:17

38: wipe that smile off your face

Now Moses was a very humble man,
more humble than anyone else
on the face of the earth.

Numbers 12:3

My son Jonah is six years old and ready for the NHL draft. Well, at least in his own mind he's ready to skate with the big boys of hockey. Could he onetime a goal from the blue line, right past Cujo (Detroit goalie Curtis Joseph)? Not a problem for Jonah. Because, as he explains, "I have a great wrist shot, Mom." Check a huge defenseman into the boards, win the face-off every time, score a hat trick on an off night? These achievements are, in my son's viewpoint, only around the corner.

Mind you, the tyke is only on his third round of skating lessons, his first with hockey equipment on, yet his ice dreams are as way out there as pies in the sky. Of course, I try to temper his completely bloated perspective by droning on about hard work and practice and getting along with your teammates. "Wayne Gretzky and his dad used to practice together all the time in their backyard rink before he really got good enough for the big leagues," I tell him.

"Can we get a rink in our backyard?" he eagerly asks. Oh sure. We'll just bulldoze the swing set and hose the whole yard down with water in the middle of winter. No big deal.

As much as my son seems to think he is the heir apparent to Eric Lindros, the real deal is that he has a very long way to go. I hate to puncture his balloon, filled as he is with the kind of dreams only a child unmarred by the realities and disappointments of life can harbor. It's not as if he thinks he's better than anyone else. Actually, he seems to believe everyone in his skating group is a mere few lace-ups away from donning their pro jerseys. I will let him figure out in the game of life, with my guidance, of course, that his first signing bonus may be a ways off.

Some parents wouldn't let their child harbor such delusions of grandeur, not even for a few minutes. By raining on their child's parade, they are saving them from a world of pain down the road, right? Maybe not. I think there needs to be a balance between allowing our children to dream big dreams and giving them the direction they need to see the sometimes hard truths of life.

Much more problematic, to my way of thinking, is when fully socialized adults think far more of themselves and their talents and virtues than they ought. We may think we are superior to other people because we have more fashionable clothes, are better educated, have more sparkling personalities, and so on; and once that notion takes root in our souls—watch out! It will grow until we *do* have the egos of a multimillion-dollar sports superstar. According to God's Word, any kind of arrogance irritates God. The command to be humble is embroidered in bold colors throughout Scripture. Take, for instance, the account of Miriam and Aaron fussing and sniping behind their brother's back that he shouldn't have married Zipporah, his Cushite wife.

God blasted them, extolling Moses's character and ultimately zapping Miriam with leprosy. (She was healed only after Moses begged on her behalf, and then after a period of seven days' exile from the camp.)

If my mini Mario ever does become too big for his britches, or shin pads as it were, he'll definitely get some action from his pa and me. We're his parents—that's our job.

God's job is to give us action when we as his children slide into thinking we may be better or more important than our brothers and sisters in Christ. "Do nothing out of selfish ambition or vain conceit, but in humility consider others better than yourself," Paul wrote to the Philippians. Memorize that verse if you haven't already, and let it be your touchstone for all your dealings with other people. Practicing humility takes lots of practice, but it is always a good plan.

God opposes the proud but gives grace to the humble.

James 4:6

39: you know better than to do that

Even a fool is thought wise if he keeps silent,
and discerning if he holds his tongue.

Proverbs 17:28

My dog—or should I say my husband's dog—drives me wacko sometimes. Among Dinah's many irritating habits is her propensity for shoving past whatever human happens to be in the front doorway and dashing away on the sidewalk, completely impervious to me bellowing, "Come back here right now, you fleabag!"

If she's wearing her collar, we may snag her and drag her back into the house. If she's not, a scruff of fur might do. But if my hands are full, as they usually are, and one of the kids opens the door to make way for our exit, Dinah often barges right past the little bodies blocking the doorway and runs off into the sunset, only to reappear an hour or two later. "She's a hound," my husband says with a shrug. "They like to run away."

Well, this was small comfort indeed when the scary dogcatcher lady showed up and offered to give our canine back if we ponied up the cash to pay the ticket she was waving in our faces. And even if the dogcatcher doesn't grab her, Dinah's jaunts into the neighborhood are fraught with potential disaster. She could get hit by a car, get into a tussle with another dog, or even bite someone, though she is—to her credit—very gentle.

The kids know that they need to be careful when opening the front door. So when Jonah recently shoved open the door and then stood there daydreaming for a minute, Dinah saw a great opportunity to scout the hood one more time. In a flash she was out the door and three houses away before I could even say, "Oops, she did it again."

"Jonah!" I scolded. "You know better than to let Dinah out like that!" He felt bad for his slip-up, and really, I blamed the dog far more than my six-year-old. Given to bouts of dreaminess (a chip off the old block—me), Jonah was lost in a moment of personal reverie and momentarily forgot the Dinah drill.

It's vexing to say the least when our kids do things they know better than to do. Potty-training regression comes to mind as one of my least favorite mess-ups. When an almost-trained child unloads under the dining room table five minutes after getting off the commode and saying he doesn't have to go, it's enough to make a mom snap like a dry twig. "You know better!" you want to yell, but you don't, because yelling at a trainee is a very, very detrimental action that could slow down the whole process for possibly years—or at least that's what the experts say. *Sigh.*

We grown-ups also goof up in areas in which we definitely know better. In fact, not half an hour after Jonah gave Dinah a "Get-Out-of-Jail-Free" card, I lost my temper in a situation in which I should have kept it. I was tired of having the babysitter's dogs jump all over me with their muddy paws every time I dropped the kids off, and instead of thinking of a tactful and constructive way to deal with it, I said something in an obviously annoyed way to the sitter. Her eyes widened in surprise, and instantly I knew I should have had more control. *You should have just let it go this time and prayed about a way to bring it up with her,* I fumed at myself on the way home. *Now it will probably be awkward with her, and you probably compromised your relationship with a good babysitter!*

I should have known better, but I didn't. We all make mistakes, even ones we have made again and again. Thank goodness for God's grace and his willingness to give us a fresh page every day.

You are a forgiving God,
gracious and compassionate,
slow to anger and abounding in love.

Nehemiah 9:17

40: you can look but you can't touch

Godliness with contentment is great gain.

1 Timothy 6:6

You've heard about the bull in the china shop? My two boys were bullish indeed during their toddler years, though we never went anywhere near a china shop. Toddlers are insatiable in their curiosity; everything must be examined and examined *now*. They also have no impulse control, so they are very grabby little critters. Thankfully, the grab-'n'-go guys at my house never smashed anything of great value, though they certainly tried. Every trip to the card shop was a stressful event, with me trying in vain to pick out a birthday card or thank-you notes or whatever while maintaining 100 percent surveillance of a rampaging thirty-five-pound person with zeal to spare. As you probably know, 100 percent surveillance is exhausting. Every time I left one of those stores, turbo toddler in tow, I felt as wilted as a dishrag.

Toddlers are also famous for their unwillingness to part with anything that may or may not be theirs. "What's mine is mine and what's yours is mine" strikes them as a slick motto. And they definitely want things that belong to other people. My cousin-in-law Alanna told me about this one slice of life in their family's history when their little Bennett would do a snatch, grab, and run like crazy routine. The tot would spy a toy in the possession of his big brother, Maxwell, size up his chances for appropriating it, then swoop down with all the finesse of a buzzard and dash to the nether regions of the house, grinning gleefully. Of course, this riled up poor Max, which was probably Ben's plan.

We adults have a little more in the way of social graces than a two-year-old, but I think we often fall into the trap of wanting what belongs to others. In our kamikaze consumer culture, we are all about who has the most chichi décor, the classiest wardrobe, and the shiniest, most loaded minivan on the cul-de-sac. I used to think I was really not jealous of some of my friends who had bigger, nicer houses and who seemed to be able to afford whatever home décor items and flourishes their hearts desired. Actually, I believed this kind of "keeping-up-with-the-Joneses" was beneath me. Then it hit me: jealousy is not beneath me! Here's how I happened to discover this news flash about myself.

The gym at which I have a membership happens to be in a tony part of town, right next to a less tony, more "Leave it to Beaver" neighborhood where I happen to live. It's definitely a luxury in my life, but I know I would never go to a gym farther away. This one happens to be the most convenient. Well, over the years I have rolled my eyes at the pretentiousness of some of my fellow members. Like the time I accidentally grabbed a black diaper bag off the nursery shelf, only to quickly discover it wasn't mine at all. I knew this, because though the bags were almost identical in make and fabric, the one I picked up by mistake had the label "Prada" on it. It was probably a four-hundred-dollar diaper bag, in contrast to mine, which was bought for twenty-two dollars at Meijer (a Wal-Mart–like department store in the

Midwest). I actually felt quite smug about it for some time, my feelings even dipping down into the contempt range for this poor, unsuspecting woman of means, whoever she is.

It's not exactly spiritual to be smug or contemptuous, either; but hey, at least I wasn't jealous of her Prada bag now, was I? Well, maybe not, but that doesn't mean I haven't harbored covetousness in my heart for some material item belonging to someone else, be it a house, furniture, or even jewelry. Sometimes I struggle to be content with my own house, living room set, or the rings on my fingers. Who cares if a diamond ring is a quarter carat or a carat, or if the setting is platinum or white gold? Really, who cares? That's a great question!

We shouldn't care too much about what kinds of goods are piling up at our neighbor's abode. We should focus instead on how God is providing for us and meeting our needs and trust him for the overall best in our lives. That is easier said than done, which is why I think "Do not covet" made God's Top Ten list back on the mountaintop with Moses. Are we willing to trust God to take care of us? Or do we think we know better, that we should have some of those goodies he has seen fit to give to our friends?

All labor and all achievement spring from
man's envy of his neighbor.
This too is meaningless,
a chasing after the wind.

Ecclesiastes 4:4

41: i love you (but you're driving me crazy)

Be imitators of God, therefore,
as dearly loved children.

Ephesians 5:1

I recently had a home kitchen party for my lovely sister-in-law. The aspect of having these kinds of parties that most stresses me out is cleaning my house. I am not going to get any medals for "Most Polished China Cabinet" or "Most Gleaming Bathroom Fixtures" from the Good Housekeeping Society. Maybe "Most Dog Hair Accumulated" or "Most Impressively Piled Stacks of Paper," but that's about it.

But dog hair can be dealt with (though our Dinah should surely go in the Guinness Book of World Records for her shedding capacity), and papers can be shoved into closets or maybe even pitched. What worried me this time as I surveyed my cluttered yet cozy abode was the crayon doodlings on the walls. Yes, I did say "walls," as in more than one wall. Somehow between the ages of one and a half and two and a half, my Ezra had managed to leave his artwork on almost every bare surface under three feet high in the entire house.

Purple squiggles, red lines, and—horrors—black alien looking guys with asymmetrical heads and eerie, oblong eyes were printed by Mr. Picasso with great zeal and joy. Where was I when these creations were being created? That's an excellent question, because I'm not entirely sure. One theory I have is that the little rabble-rouser got busy every time I was in the shower, but only he and his Maker really know for sure.

No amount of discipline, carefully and firmly applied, seemed to impress upon the mad artiste that coloring on walls was a bad, very bad, endeavor. Noooo siree. I tried everything: hiding the crayons, providing him with sheaves of white paper, and scolding didn't seem to do the trick. *Well,* I thought, *at least the crayon will come off with some cleanser and elbow grease.* Nope. It wasn't coming off, no way, no how.

But just when we thought our only recourse was to repaint the walls, Mr. Clean came out with Magic Eraser, a product so fantastic and timely that I would surely kiss Mr. Clean's shiny bald head if I had the chance. Magic Eraser, you see, gets out crayon like nothing else. The unfortunate ink-pen squiggles weren't budging, but after I muscled my way through wall after wall with my miracle product, the house did look about 90 percent better.

On the day of the party, with candles lit and flowers arranged, I thought with some satisfaction that my home really did look pretty spiffy. Do you know what's coming next? Disaster! In the form of newly discovered drawings on my freshly scrubbed walls—in *ink pen.* The Artist Formerly Known as Ezra (now known as "Dead Meat") had fallen off the inappropriate doodling wagon and had committed a very grave crime against his mother and Mr. Clean.

I don't know if I've ever been so angry at one of my kids. Smoke was coming out of my ears! I told his father to deal with him because I was just too stomping, spittin' mad. Did I like my child at that moment? Not even a little bit. Was I disgusted with his behavior? Oh yeah, girlfriend, you know it. But did I still love him? Oddly enough, yes. The love I had for my little stinker was so deeply rooted that even a travesty like fresh ink drawings on the night of a fancy chick party wasn't enough to make me stop. And I'm so grateful God loves me unconditionally, even when I commit the same crime against him again and again. And I'm awed too that his blood is enough to miraculously wipe away every trace of what I've done!

Your love, O LORD, reaches to the heavens,
your faithfulness to the skies.
Psalm 36:5

42: you were born in my heart

In love, he predestined us to be adopted as sons through Jesus Christ.

Ephesians 1:5

"You were born in my heart," my mom would tell my brother and me when we were little. "Some babies grow in their mother's tummy, but you grew in my heart, and you were born there too." People who are the biological daughters and sons of their parents sometimes don't understand that an adopted child feels the same way as they do. Well, most adopted children do. I always did, and do, that I know for sure.

My birth mother was a young teacher at a Catholic school, twenty-one years old and all but estranged from her mother. As a result of a summer fling, she became pregnant with me. No one in her family was told of her pregnancy, and only her roommate and her employer at a new office job (Catholic teachers did not publicly become pregnant out of wedlock in the late sixties, and she had to quit her teaching job) knew of her condition.

My birth father, before being told his girlfriend was pregnant, abruptly broke up with her. She believes to this day that he found out the news from his roommate, who happened to be dating her roommate. At any rate, Christine was all alone in the world. When she went into labor, she called herself a taxi to get to the hospital. Another cab was called a few days later, after she had given birth and sufficiently healed to be sent back to her apartment. Alone and mourning her empty arms, Christine had to grit her teeth and get through each day. The first few weeks she stuffed Saran Wrap in her bra because she was leaking so much, a grim reminder that she had just been through the most wrenching loss of her life.

The only thing that got her through was her hope that I was going to be given to a loving couple. When I finally, as a twenty-seven-year-old, learned her story, I felt terrible she had gone through so much all alone.

Yet I knew then and know now that God had guided Christine's story, and my story, and the story of the childless couple he planned for me. From the foundations of time, he orchestrated for me to be born from that messy and ill-fated summer romance and to be adopted by Abe and Linda Reimer. My parents had been married four years when they brought me into their home. They never found out why they couldn't have children, and it was just as well. God opened their hearts to adoption in a time when it was quite foreign indeed. People would sometimes make remarks to my mom like, "Oh, so *this* is how you get your children," and other snide, useless comments. When people would misunderstand or treat me differently, it would cut her to the quick. But gradually their family and friends adjusted to my novel arrival in their midst. In fact, other young couples took their cue and adopted babies of their own.

My brother, Dan, and I were always told that our birth mothers loved us and gave us away so that we could have a life with two parents who wanted us, who couldn't have children. And we were told that we were loved by them just as much as if we had been the joint result of their DNA. There are so many miracles in adoption. One is how adopted children often start to look like their parents, though there is no biological basis for it. My parents are short people. My dad has more short jokes up his short sleeve than a stand-up comedian. I'm average height with brown hair and blue eyes. But my brother towers over us all. Danish by blood, Dan is six feet, four inches tall with chiseled features and watery grayish blue eyes and blond hair. He looks like a Viking straight off the boat from Iceland. Our college friends, though, never failed to comment on how we looked alike. The Reimer family, they said, had a "look" about them that strongly suggested we were all related. Of course, we *are* related, just not in the way people think we are! It's just one more way God has knit the four of us as a family.

Now that Doyle and I are in the process of adopting a baby girl, I've been thinking so much about adoption. The spiritual parallels are rich and beautiful! God also planned, from the foundations of time, that you and I would be adopted as his daughters, spliced into the family film, with our names written in the family scrapbook, the Book of Life. I hope people think that, just like I somehow look like my Viking brother, I also bear resemblance to the Father who chose me, eons ago, to be his beloved child.

Rejoice greatly, O Daughter of Zion!
Shout, daughter of Jerusalem.

Zechariah 9:9

43: there are starving children in africa

A generous man will himself be blessed, for he shares his food with the poor.

Proverbs 22:9

Is there anything more disheartening than a child who turns up his nose at perfectly good and probably delicious food? It drives me bananas when my kids kvetch about the food Doyle or I have prepared (or ordered). *They have no idea how privileged they really are,* I think. Of course, when I feel compelled to use the old "Some kids have no food at all, so you should be happy you have yummy and good-for-you things to eat," it falls about as flat as when I was given a similar speech as an ungrateful wretch of a child. "So send it to them," I would say, half-joking, to my poor mother, upon being lectured about the empty stomachs of girls and boys across the world. And raised as I was by an immigrant dad who often had only tulip bulbs and thistles to keep hunger pangs at bay, I really wasn't a child completely out of touch with the reality of poverty and hardship. I myself didn't know that kind of deprivation, but I heard enough stories about my dad's family that I had a sense of knowledge and compassion for those who went without. Yet I still made snarky comments like "Send it to them!"

It *is* frustrating when our incredibly well-fed children don't seem to know or care that so many of their peers are hungry and malnourished. There has to be a way for us as Christians and mothers to impart a sense of concern to our children for those who are less fortunate. The Scriptures are woven throughout with commands to give to the poor and help the disenfranchised find justice and stability. Proverbs 21:13 says, "If a man shuts his eyes to the cry of the poor, he too will cry out and not be answered."

A good first step in imparting this value to our tots is to drive home the point that not everyone on the planet—or even within a couple of miles around them—have as much as they do. One great idea I heard was from a book called *Stuffed Animals on the Ceiling Fan* by Silvana Clark. Listen to this:

> I was fed up with my eight-year-old and ten-year-old constantly picking at their food and demanding special meals. So one Friday afternoon I cleaned out the refrigerator of all leftovers and froze whatever I could. I also packed up all the cookies and treats from the snack cupboard. When my children came home from school, I calmly explained that this weekend we were going to eat like people in Third World countries ate. Their eyes widened in shock as I explained there would be no snacks and only rice and water for dinner. Saturday morning breakfast consisted only of complaints and more rice. By lunch my kids were cranky but I hung in there and served rice. Dinner was a treat with rice and one apple, shared among the four of us. Sunday breakfast consisted of one piece of dry toast and a tiny glass of milk each. At noon my kids were very hungry. While eating their bowls of plain rice, I explained how tired I was of them being picky eaters. From now on, they had a choice of eating what I served, or they could have a bowl of rice. It worked. We had very few complaints from then on.[7]

Extreme? Kind of, but I can see how this little plan could work wonders in imbuing gratitude and hopefully generosity in a child. Here are some other ideas for cultivating compassion:

Sponsor a child your child's age in a Third World country through an organization like Compassion International.

Volunteer together at a soup kitchen or mission.

As a family project, pack up a shoe box full of small toys, hygiene items, and school supplies for a Samaritan's Purse Christmas drive, or fill a box with food and deliver it together to a family in need.

When grocery shopping, buy a few extra cans of soup or stew and tell your child they are for a child who doesn't have enough to eat; then donate the canned goods to a food pantry.

When we intentionally enlighten our kids that they are not—shocker!—the center of the free world, and each follower of Christ is required to do his or her part for those in need, we can get past our kids' selfishness and our own to a place of giving and kindness.

Even in darkness light dawns for the upright,
for the gracious and compassionate and righteous man. . . .
He has scattered abroad his gifts to the poor.

Psalm 112:4, 9

44: because i'm your mother, that's why

Who has measured the waters in the hollow of his hand, or with the breadth of his hand marked off the heavens?

Isaiah 40:12

Sometimes the only answer I can think of is this: "Because I'm your mother, that's why!" I try not to use it too often, because I think it exasperates my munchkins. Yes, they should recognize my authority and comply meekly with my wishes, but often the little donkeys want to know *why*.

Why the big one can't buy new knee pads and shin guards.

Why the little one can't have gummy worms for breakfast.

Why they both must submit to nail clipping every so often even though they loathe it.

These are all things grown-ups understand but little ones find unbelievably difficult to grasp.

On a much grander scale, God is the Grown-up, and we are the little donkeys, braying up a storm when we don't quite understand where he is going with something. Hey, it makes sense to us that he would do it this way, so why is he doing it another way?

I bet once in a while our God looks down and gently but firmly says, "Because I'm your Father, that's why."

Sometimes, with the passage of time, comes new understanding, and God gives us a glimpse of what he was up to back when we couldn't figure out his ways. My friend Joanne and her family recently went through a journey like this. In their late forties, John and Joanne were done with babies—or so they thought. Their clan consisted of four daughters—two biological daughters, Taylor and Shelby, who are in their teens, and two adopted daughters, Mackenzie, nine, and Sydney, five. The motto of the Swart tribe seemed to be "Girls just wanna have fun."

And then they got the call that would change their lives.

Sydney's birth mother, the social worker told them, was pregnant with another baby, a boy, and she and the birth father wanted John and Joanne to adopt him. In the past the Swarts had received a few calls from the adoption agency asking if they might be interested in another child for their beautiful, multiracial family that already included daughters of African American and Chinese heritage. They always prayed about each baby, and it had never seemed to be God's intent for them to pursue another adoption.

But this baby was different. For one thing, he was Syd's biological brother, and that was very compelling to them. Mostly, though, they felt a sense that God was opening their hearts to this child. They agreed to take the baby, and the Swart women (and John) were beside themselves with excitement over bringing home their baby brother. An adorable, itty-bitty boy wardrobe was assembled with great glee, and church friends and family members started unloading all manner of used baby equipment. Everyone who knew and loved this family was swept up in the thrill of this precious baby joining their clan.

On the day the baby was born, the Swarts were literally installing the car seat when they got a call saying that the birth mother had changed her mind. She took the baby home with her from the hospital.

John and Joanne and the girls were devastated. They already loved this wee one as their own. It made absolutely no sense whatsoever why this would happen. Hadn't they felt a great peace about adopting this child?

But God knew what he was doing. He had given the family peace and had opened their hearts to the prospect of a newcomer, a baby boy. He had even outfitted their home with the necessary clothes and furniture and whatnot to accommodate an infant. But instead of Sydney's birth brother, God had another boy in mind. Two months after their great disappointment, the Swarts received yet one more phone call from the social worker. A seven-week-old baby boy, half African American and half Nigerian, had become available for adoption. His birth parents had signed off on their parental rights, and there was no chance of them changing their minds. Were they still interested in adopting a son? Well, they couldn't get their hands on that gorgeous baby fast enough! God intended all along for Jackson Elijah Athanasius to be a Swart, to have four doting big sisters and parents who are tickled pink to get up with him at night. Really!

"Because I'm your Father, that's why." Next time we're confused about what God is doing in our lives, let's remember he always has a good reason. We just have to trust that.

I will come and proclaim your mighty acts,
O Sovereign Lord.
Psalm 71:16

45: be nice to your brother

But if we walk in the light, as he is in the light,
we have fellowship with one another.

1 John 1:7

"Why?" my son Jonah implored. "Why should I be nice to Ez when all he does is wreck my stuff and bug me all the time?"

"Jo Jo, I know it's really hard to be nice to someone who isn't always nice to you," I started.

"You mean someone who is *never* nice to you," Jonah interjected, grumbling.

"Well, whatever. You know your brother is nice to you most of the time. But anyway, it's important to be kind to your brother because you will always have each other. Even if your friends aren't there for you, you'll always have your brother. You two will stick together through all kinds of stuff, good and bad."

Of course, this little lecture didn't appear to have any instant results. Jonah was still steamed that his fractious confrere had colored on his library book (so was I, for that matter), but I hoped that the message had soaked in at least a little.

Every time I deliver this speech I get this strange feeling that I'm turning into my father. Born in Ukraine, my dad's childhood was filled with war, terror, and upheaval. The only constant he had was his family, so even when his life stabilized drastically upon immigrating to Canada, he always clung to family.

I was always a "friend" kind of person, more into my posse of gal pals than getting together with uncles and aunts and cousins with whom I had little in common. Somehow my Mennonite uncles didn't groove on discussing the new videos on *Friday Night Videos* (the Total Request Live of the eighties). Go figure! So for years I would roll my eyes when my dad would give his "the family is number one" speech.

But as time went by and I moved beyond the relatively shallow concerns of a teenager, I began to see that dear old Dad had a point. Even though I have lifelong friends whom I treasure and love dearly, I do value the bonds of kinship much more than I used to. Only my brother truly understands the unique ups and downs of being raised in our household, and only he loves my parents as much as I do.

As I grow and mature in my faith, I also increasingly see the value of unity in the family of God. Our Father urges us in his Word to be in fellowship with our spiritual brothers and sisters, to love them and be devoted to them just like family.

I'm adopted, so the many references to adoption in Scripture really resonate with me, such as Ephesians 1:5: "In love, he predestined us to be adopted as his sons through Jesus Christ, in accordance with his pleasure and will."

I know firsthand the profound beauty of being grafted into a new family tree, then sharing the same roots as if I was never a separate branch. As believers, we are all adopted, once-individual branches now forever entwined in a covenant of love with one common Father. When we obey God's commands to love, defer to, and encourage and uplift one another, all because of our mutual devotion to our heavenly Parent, we really become like a family.

This truth was brought home to me last summer when the members of our small group came together and acted as next of kin for one of our own. Dear Marge, a seventy-six-year-old woman whom we called "Grandma Marge," lost her daughter suddenly to heart failure. Marge's other children were unable to help for one reason or another, so it fell to us, her church family, to plan a funeral for a woman we barely knew. I even ended up going to the mall to buy a dress for Joyce to wear in the coffin. That was a one-of-a-kind shopping trip! But her funeral was one of the most amazing, blessed experiences I've ever had. Every little sacrifice people made, and each small but loving gesture made on Marge's behalf underscored the fact that we were her family and she was ours. And family, as I heard a million times growing up, is number one.

A new command I give you: Love one another.
As I have loved you, so you must love one another.
By this all men will know that you are my disciples,
if you love one another.

John 13:34–35

46: cough into your sleeve

So then, dear friends, since you are looking forward to this, make every effort to be found spotless, blameless and at peace with him.

2 Peter 3:14

As one who hails from the coldest city in the world, Winnipeg, Manitoba—we even have T-shirts that say that!—I've always prided myself on being Winter Woman. I love hockey, ice skating, tobogganing, snowman building, and snowball throwing. Because I became acclimatized to extreme cold (Winnipeg can get to minus fifty degrees in the dead of winter), I usually walk around in the Michigan winters with my coat flapping open, hands bare, and head free of the knit hats my friends don every time the weather dips below zero. Yes, people think I'm a bit dotty, but it never occurs to me to dress for the cold weather if it's not the arctic blast I'm used to.

"You'll catch your death of cold," I've been told more than once. Well, we all know that's an old wives' tale. You don't contract colds or the flu from the chill in the air or from wiping snow off your car. The reason we usually come down with the creeping crud once or twice a winter is because we're all inside, and the germs that cause illness are congregating inside with us. When we use the pay phone, ATM, debit card machine—whatever—we're risking our health.

I don't know about you, but every year at our house we get a round or two of the four-day family flu. You know, the one where everyone in the house is competing for the toilet or lying in a feverish clump, sneezing and coughing up a storm. It only takes one kid bringing home a virus from preschool before the whole family starts to drop like flies. With my clan, one sneeze is grounds for suspicion, and two *ha-choo*s means it's all over: within half a day the sneezer will be down for the count.

It's enough to make even the most diehard Winter Women, such as myself, long for summer days, when at least my family stands a chance of making it through a couple of weeks in a robust state of health. The specter of getting sick is also sufficient grounds for becoming a germ-phobic. Aside from pushing vitamins like some crazy woman, I also go a little nuts with disinfecting door handles, phone receivers, and other surfaces that may harbor the bug du jour. I carry along a little container of instant hand sanitizer in case my fingers come in contact with icky-looking elevator buttons or whatever—not that germs are visible anyway, but, well, a picture is worth a thousand words. If it looks icky, it must be icky—am I right?

I also drill into my children's heads the preeminence of germ control, which starts with the habit of not sneezing into the atmosphere but rather into a Kleenex, ideally, or if they must, a sleeve.

"But mom, I can't control my sneezes!" my kindergarten man will protest.

"Just try and control them a little," I'll say. "Shut your mouth anyway if you can, and make it a 'dry sneeze.'"

"But mom! Justin from my class says his dad says those kind of sneezes where you squeeze them in make your brain cells die!" Now the kid looks completely appalled, as if I am suggesting he drink bleach or something.

Well, what's a few lost brain cells compared to four people capsized by the flu? These thoughts are private, of course, because there's no chance of winning an argument like this against Justin, He Who Knows All, and his father. No, the important thing is to keep up the campaign against germs, to continue fiendish hand-washing and vigilant eye-balling of potentially infectious surfaces.

Bad habits can snowball in the same way germs do, and they are just as catchy. I'm not talking about drinking a swig of milk out of the milk carton, although that's probably how some of these viruses get going at our house. I'm referring to insidious little corruptions and doings that can infect us and make us spiritually sluggish, malaise-ridden, and maybe exposed to something worse. Let's take jealousy, for example. Or lust. Gossip. Temptations or attitudes that at first flit through our souls, then stay longer, eventually contaminating our spirits.

If we spent half the time and energy guarding our hearts and minds as we do our bodies from germs, we'd be thoroughly inoculated, strong and vibrantly healthy, and ready to fight any spiritual bacteria that came our way.

Be on your guard; stand firm in the faith.

1 Corinthians 16:13

47: pick up your toys

Let us throw off everything that hinders
and the sin that so easily entangles.

Hebrews 12:1

Sometimes I just know I will meet my Maker as a result of tripping on a Matchbox car. Yes, I can see it all unfold: I will be traipsing along, probably carrying a load of folded towels, when my foot will descend on one of those insidious little vehicles. I will skid for a second as my life flashes before my eyes, towels flying everywhere as I lose my balance, legs akimbo, and land on my head, a three-inch steel Corvette imbedded in my cranium. One minute I'll be leisurely going about my duties, and the next I'll be with the saints in Glory Land.

The reason this vision is so crisp in my mind is because I've nearly bought the farm many a time as I have navigated our none-too-big home and tried to avoid the flotsam and jetsam of life with small children. Either this scenario will develop, I postulate, or else I will trip over Dinah, the part-mule basset hound, or Tallulah, the cat who seems to be underfoot more than anywhere else. Either way, the clutter around here is hazardous to my health.

Making sure the pathways are clear doesn't seem to be too high on anyone's priority list. My kids eschew the nooks and crannies that are meant for playing and drawing and plop themselves smack dab in the middle of the hall or right in the entranceway to the house or maybe even on the stairs. And picking up their toys is also an unpopular activity.

"Do I have to?"

"Yes."

"I didn't even make that mess!"

"Yup, you did. You just forgot about it two messes ago."

"Why can't I just leave it there until next time I play with it?"

"Oy vey!"

This is always a sore spot for me, and not because I'm a neat freak. Oh no, it's just the opposite. As a child, my very domestic mom usually picked up after me because she had high standards for neatness and order. Somehow this worked out well for my brother, whose sock drawer is organized with military precision. But for me? Well, let's just say I won't win any housekeeping awards anytime soon. I have a great mom, but in some ways her willingness to serve her family and maintain an orderly home for us backfired, because I didn't really learn to pick up after myself properly. Now that I have kids, it is not second nature to get them to clean up their toys. Actually, I can see the beauty of my mother's way: it's far easier to pick up their toys for them than to make them do it themselves.

But I know it is better for them if they have to take responsibility for their own messes. So most of the time I grit my teeth and make it mandatory for my boys to pick up their toys. The writer of Hebrews says, "Let us throw off everything that hinders and the sin that so easily entangles." Like little cars strewn on the stairs, or pieces of drawing paper abandoned in the middle of the kitchen floor, so our bad habits and spiritual ruts can make us trip and slip.

In this same passage, our faith journey is compared to a running contest. "Let us run with perseverance the race marked out for us." The clutter in our lives can distract us from focusing on Jesus and his plans for us. Satan uses the sin we hold on to with great efficiency, tangling our feet on the path and causing us to stumble and fall. If unchecked, sins can accumulate and cause all sorts of problems. Our focus is lost, our vision blurred, and God's best for us is compromised.

It is in my kids' best interest that they are required to put away the Candyland pieces before they break out the Junior Monopoly box. Those games are way more fun—and make much more sense—when all their individual pieces are in their proper places, not jumbled in a mishmash of cards and pieces.

Picking up the litter in our hearts by admitting what we've done and asking for forgiveness means we can traverse the path set before us in safety. And instead of being delayed by the "hindrances" and "entanglements," we can run like the wind toward the one who loves us.

If we confess our sins, he is faithful and just
and will forgive us our sins and purify us
from all unrighteousness.

1 John 1:9

48: shhh, mommy's on the phone

Go in peace, for we have sworn friendship
with each other in the name of the LORD, saying,
"The LORD is witness between you and me,
and between your descendants
and my descendants forever."

1 Samuel 20:43

I know a woman who says, whenever she's on the phone, her five children cluster around her like a bunch of clucking chickens. "It doesn't matter if all five of them are watching a video, totally occupied. If they see that I'm on the phone, they will follow me to the attic. All of a sudden they need juice, cereal, a snack, a stray sock, or the whereabouts of our pet lizard. It's truly unbelievable."

I personally welcome the intrusion of my kids if I'm dealing with, say, a guy who wants to sell me siding or magazine subscriptions. But if it's a girlfriend I'm chatting with, I mind a whole lot more. Girlfriends are true sanity savers in my wipe-a-nose day. They lift my spirits when I've had a rough potty-training episode. They share tips about teething or tantrums. They make me laugh and take me outside myself.

My buddies Rachel and Mary Jo and I have had some amazing girlfriends' getaways over the years. We once spent New Year's Eve at a swanky restaurant in Chicago, but that was before I had my first baby. Après Jonah a weekender with pals became an undertaking of massive proportions. We did swing a day trip to Ann Arbor last summer, and I very much enjoyed eating at a restaurant where chicken nuggets and hotdogs weren't on the menu. But now Mary Jo has a toddler, and I have a kindergartner and a three-year-old. Rachel, who just got married this summer, could take off and do the weekends and day trips by herself if she wanted, but what fun would that be?

Life sure has changed since the three of us could go to chick flicks on the spur of the moment, leisurely sip lattes while chatting about fabulous reads, and shop for open-toed sandals—in a size 7. Now we're at different places on the continuum of life, which means it has become more and more of a challenge to stay connected.

Friendships undergo dramatic transformations when we become parents. Writer Paula Spencer says, "That's because the kind of support and socializing you need evolves along with your baby, as does the amount of free time you have and how you want to spend it."

You already know this: having kids has reshaped your relationships. You will win some chums, lose some, and grow closer to others. There are barriers to overcome with any friendship. But when we're wrapped up in a world of potty training and baby sign language, we need our amigos more than ever.

Moms tend to glom on to each other and get lost in their own little world, but I think it's key to maintain—or cultivate—some connections with nonmommy pals. Friendships with singles can be hard to maintain, but I remain a huge fan. It can be refreshing to hear exotic stories from Planet Infantless about blind dates, job promotions, and travel. ("You actually drank tomato juice on the airplane, and you weren't wearing it by the end?")

Then there's your gal pals who are married with no kids yet, or maybe ever for reasons of choice or—sticky wickets here—infertility. These scenarios throw up similar barriers to your ties to solo girlfriends. Keeping these relationships strong will take some elbow grease, patience, and sensitivity on your end to fuel the friendship, but don't ditch your kidless confidantes.

The hardest thing is to find common ground. What brought you together in the first place? Not babies, that's for sure. But there's more to you than kids, believe it or not. There's your faith journey, music, books, a sport or hobby, a similar wacky sense of humor, a shared history, or something else. Focus on these things. *Especially* when your friend is enduring the pain of infertility, be sure to keep baby stories to a minimum.

Above all, show your nonmommy friends they matter. Remember birthdays, ask about the date with the drummer—or sympathize if one of your friends has had a hideous breakup. Return calls and emails. Variety is the spice of life, and sustaining relationships with friends who may not have tons in common with you anymore is a stretching, positive thing.

A friend loves at all times.

Proverbs 17:17

49: to have a friend you must be a friend

Perfume and incense bring joy to the heart,
and the pleasantness of one's friend
springs from earnest counsel.

Proverbs 27:9

One of my longtime friends, Bonnie, and I didn't seem to have much to talk about during the five years when she had kids and I didn't. An older, wiser mom told me to give it time. "Just wait until you have your first baby," she said. "You and Bonnie will never run out of things to say again." This wise mom was right. Motherhood, it seems, is the ultimate bonding agent.

But as fun as it is to ride the same wavelength as the mom gang, beware of that big spoiler, competitiveness. "Oh, wee Moe is small for his age? Well, that's a shame, isn't it? My Archie is off the charts for weight and height," Ms. Ain't-We-Grand confides smugly. *Ouch!* We are so gaga over our babies and so wholly devoted to their well-being that even the remotest sign that another child may be more advanced makes the mother bear in us roar in defensive protest.

Moms compete in a multitude of ways, from the breastfeeding and bottle-feeding dilemma, to developmental milestones, and later on, in our education choices. Many friendships have bit the dust over issues like this. What a shame, because your fellow mom friends can truly help you through rough passages of raising kids like no other friends can. "Two are better than one, because they have a good return for their work," Solomon said in Ecclesiastes. "If one falls down, [her] friend can help [her] up. . . . Though one may be overpowered, two can defend themselves. A cord of three strands is not quickly broken" (Eccles. 4:9–10, 12). When you're having a messy stretch of life with your children, a friend who understands you, supports you, holds your hand, and lifts you up—literally and otherwise—is truly a gift from God.

So don't let a pal's competitive comments fracture your friendship. Try to receive these remarks with a grain of salt, because sometimes mommy arrogance masks a deeper insecurity.

If an amigo of yours is driving you nuts with her constant comparisons, you have a few choices. If she's an acquaintance or a "fringe friend," blow it off. Life's too short to have a cow over an insensitive statement. But if the friend's competitive remarks are making you feel like a rival instead of a friend, it's time to tactfully confront her. "When you say things like that, it makes me feel defensive. I mean, all kids do things in their own time, so can't we just enjoy our kids and leave it at that? Yes, your Connor is an early reader, which is great, but my Jadon is really strong socially. They both have wonderful qualities." She may be shocked, or worse, come back with a "My, aren't you touchy!" comment. Take a deep breath and try to let the dust settle with a little room for both of you to evaluate your friendship. It may not survive, but at least you've expressed yourself honestly and graciously.

Another buddy barrier that comes up often on the playground or at mother and child playdates is different parenting styles.

Your friend may be incredibly strict ("no refined white flour for Lulu-belle!") while you're a laissez faire family manager, or vice versa. The key here is to remember that we all have our pet sticking points. Personally, I'm horrified by hot dogs and drivers who talk on their cell phones. But my friends who do serve Oscar Mayer once a day and jabber on their cells while tooling in their minivans would probably be appalled that I allow my children to watch certain cartoons on a regular basis. Try and maintain a "live and let live" attitude with your friends and their sometimes dissonant mommy "rules." Only if your child is truly at risk in some way—for example, your pal's wild toddler wants to play with bleach and mom doesn't care—should you say something, and then only prayerfully and with tact.

Do your best to hurdle obstacles between you and your friends. You need them so much! Pray for wisdom in handling tense situations, and stick close to buddies who are full of grace and humor. They will make your mothering journey an even richer experience.

[She] who walks with the wise grows wise.

Proverbs 13:20

50: mommy and daddy are having "quiet time"

I am my lover's and my lover is mine.

Song of Songs 6:3

Passion after parenthood can be an incredibly elusive venture. First, there's the whole matter of giving birth, pain, sleep deprivation, our brains addled with hormones that make us want to do anything but the act that got us there in the first place. Six weeks to resume having sex? Ha! More like six years. Mom and Dad may actually get back to intimacy within a few weeks or months, but it can take what seems like eons to recapture the true passion and focus one possessed before becoming a parent.

Even after the physical damages of pregnancy are healed, there's severe narcolepsy (Sleep or sex? Duh!), the odd asexual feeling as somebody's mother, and that obstacle of obstacles: privacy! You know what I mean if you've ever had a pair of little eyes gaping at you while in the middle of a romantic interlude. Door locks come in handy, but sometimes they don't even keep out unwanted intrusions. I know one set of parents who were determined to get in a quickie before the husband went away on a three-week trip, only to have all five of their children stacked like firewood outside their door wailing that they needed Mommy!

It's amazing how the pitter-patter of little feet conspire to stomp all over the activity that led to their births. But passion between parents, though challenging, is vital to a healthy marriage and thus a strong family. We are created to be sexual beings, to express our sexuality within the bond of marriage.

Not everyone is enthusiastic about making love, though. Many young mothers would rather fall out of an airplane than do the bedroom-based mattress mambo. If you fall under that category, it's time to go on a mission to rebuild your desire. Make passion a priority, cultivate your sexuality by flirting, kissing, and throwing those maternity underwear out the window! Carve out regular times to be together and connect as two people in love, not just roommates who happen to be raising the same set of children. Go out on dates, park the kids at Grandma and Grandpa's for the weekend, and discover again why sparks flew between the two of you. (Hint: it sure wasn't because you shared a similar potty-training philosophy!)

Here's a wondrous truth: God wants you to have a thrilling sex life! Just read Song of Songs all the way through. You'll blush. You'll wonder what the deal is with all the references to pomegranates and whatnot. And you'll know I'm right!

Ask God to help you rejuvenate your interest in sex if it's lacking. And call the man in your life and tell him he's "radiant and ruddy, outstanding among ten thousand" (Song of Songs 5:10) or something along those lines. He'll get the picture fast.

For this reason a man will leave his father and mother
and will be united to his wife,
and the two will become one flesh.

Ephesians 5:31

51: mommy needs a nap

Let the beloved of the LORD rest secure in him,
for he shields her all day long, and the one the
LORD loves rests between his shoulders.

Deuteronomy 33:12

Why is it that kids resist naps with all the might of their flinty wills, and meanwhile we would love nothing more than just to snuggle down with a blankie someplace and drool for an hour or two? Children also contest bedtime. If one of my boys actually admits he's tired, I know for sure he's coming down with the cold bug du jour.

Sleep is essential for optimum mothering. Without it we lose perspective, lose patience, lose humor, and just plain lose it. But even when we are getting our requisite hours of shut-eye, our souls need rest just as much as our bodies do.

Rest from wiping noses, breaking up skirmishes, kissing ouchies, answering questions about why the sky is not purple, and cutting little people's meat. Rest from the constant noise of our culture, the TV or radio blaring, the sounds of ambulances and traffic, and even people in our house talking. Rest from too much information, too many demands, and too much to cram into our day.

How can we carve out the kind of rest our souls and minds need? By intentionally creating it. Go to bed an hour earlier and just be quiet with your own thoughts and prayers. Soak in the tub. Turn on a fan for white noise and go to your bedroom while the kids are watching a movie. Even half an hour will do the trick. Turn off the TV, the radio, and the phone. Put down that wonderful novel that has kept you up half the week. Shut the glossy magazine that came in the mail. Shut your eyes, take a deep breath, and *rest.*

This may not be possible every day, but when you feel like the pet rodent, spinning for hours on his exercise wheel, it's time to step back, slow down, and find quietude, calm, and repose. I love what Deuteronomy 33:12 says: "The one the LORD loves rests between his shoulders." Like a sheep that has had enough tromping all over the place, that has walked too far and too long to find water or pasture, we can experience the kind of comfort our Father designed us to need, resting between his strong, all-powerful shoulders.

We weren't created to run on fumes for very long. Take time to rest between your Father's shoulders. Ask him to help you create balance in your life and time for rejuvenating soul downtime.

My soul finds rest in God alone.

Psalm 62:1

52: mommy's locked in the bathroom

Let us not become weary in doing good,
for at the proper time we will reap a harvest
if we do not give up.

Galatians 6:9

We've all had days when we wonder why we ever had kids, for clearly we were cut out to be turnip farmers or bank presidents, not mothers. My own "Black Thursday" unfurled recently, hour upon hour of precious little good, mostly bad, and sometimes ugly.

The day was launched on a sour note when—horror of horrors—the alarm failed to go off. I had half an hour to drag my son out of bed and whip him into presentable shape for a day of kindergarten. Have I mentioned I'm not a morning person? Well, neither is he, the little chip off the old narcoleptic block. This is why I secretly empathize with him, but that still doesn't make the mornings go any sweeter.

Literally dragging him at times—there was no time for any savvy maneuvers that morning!—through dressing, toothbrushing, breakfast, backpack detail, and so on, I was plumb tuckered out by the time he ambled out the door.

Then there was Mr. Chipper's little brother to deal with. In the midst of potty training, Ez chose to poop several times in his training pants—and the bathtub, of course! He refused to take a nap, which meant I had no precious hour to regain my sanity. My Morning Glory came home from school and blew a gasket upon being told it was time for "quiet time." (He has one every day, but on this day he decided he was extra-vehemently opposed!) Brightynn from down the street began to ring the doorbell just then, providing a decidedly manic soundtrack to my unraveling wits. Wanting to be kind, and knowing that was not an option if I opened the door, I let her continue ringing (the kid has major doorbell ringing stamina too) until she simply gave up and trotted home.

Naturally, my husband called with the news that he had to work late and asked if he could bring anything home. "Yes," I told him. "Bags and bags of chocolate."

You've been there too, I know. Every mom has been stretched to her snapping point, brought to the realization that she would gladly walk on glass for the chance to be alone in a quiet room. During those moments of despair, the only thing to do is cry out for help to the God who is always there. *"Father God, I love these kids of mine—I just can't stand them right now. Help me be patient, and help me get through this horrible day without throwing both of them and myself in a snowbank!"* That's the kind of foxhole prayer I send up at times like these, an SOS for divine intervention.

God wants to hold us together when we're falling apart. Call out to him, and be assured that he hears you and loves you and that help is on the way!

Even youths grow tired and weary,
and young [moms] stumble and fall;
but those who hope in the Lord will renew their strength.

Isaiah 40:30

53: now tell me how you're *really* feeling

You haven't been honest either with me or about me—not the way my friend Job has. . . . My friend Job will pray for you, and I will accept his prayer.

Job 42:7–8 Message

Kids are not shy about venting their frustrations or passionately giving voice to their likes and dislikes. My son Jonah loathes lima beans. The way he carries on when a few are set before him, you'd think every night was Lima Bean Casserole night. With great drama, he chews his six despicable beans slowly, tortuously, until—wonder of wonders!—those bad boys are down his gullet.

My point—and I do have one—is that even though it's a bit obnoxious to complain about a meal prepared with love by Mom or Dad, at least we know exactly where he stands on the matter. As a matter of fact, there aren't too many issues over which he bobs and weaves. Kids are known for their frankness, and that's one of the reasons we know our kids so well.

Adults, naturally, are socialized to be coy and unforthcoming, to hide their true feelings, as if risking exposure would somehow hurt or alienate the person we're talking with. The art of subtlety is not a bad thing—after all, Aunt Mildred doesn't really need to know what you think of her famous triple-decker Jell-O salad, now does she? But when we're always trying to be tactful and sensitive, we're not being completely honest, and we're not being real.

God's best friends in Scripture were often very real with him about their feelings, citing complaints, second-guessing his plans, and arguing and even wrestling with their Maker. But instead of zapping his rather fractious buddies for their insolence, God seems to encourage candor in his friends. Job was allowed to vent his bitterness during his ordeal, and in the end, God defended Job for being honest and rebuked Job's friends for being inauthentic. Abraham, Ruth, David, Jeremiah—all these faithful servants of God were allowed to let loose with their genuine emotions.

In his book *The Purpose-Driven Life*, Rick Warren says the following about our God: "Genuine friendship is built on disclosure. What may appear as *audacity* God views as *authenticity*. God listens to the passionate words of his friends; he is bored with predictable, pious clichés. To be God's friend, you must be honest to God, sharing your true feeling, not what you think you ought to feel or say."

Our children are free with their true feelings, and we know them incredibly well because of it. It's one more way God wants us to be childlike, because when we tell him how we feel, he knows us better, and our friendship with him increases.

Come near to God and he will come near to you.

James 4:8

54: leave your sister alone

Don't have anything to do with
foolish or stupid arguments,
because you know they produce quarrels.

2 Timothy 2:23

There's nothing like a good sibling smackdown to really put a dent in your day.

"She stole my hair barrette," a voice wails from the room two sisters share.

"Did not!"

"Did too!"

And on and on the yowling chorus goes until Mom ends her phone conversation (or gets out of the luxuriously hot and relaxing shower she was having), tromps upstairs, and plays referee.

Sometimes these little tiffs go poof as quickly as they were started. As my husband says, "No blood, no foul." But at other times the pain inflicted is quite real, and the hurt feelings take a while to heal.

I didn't have a sister growing up to fight over clothes with, but my brother made up for any lack of conflict on that front very nicely. Two-and-a-half years apart, we bickered vigorously over space in the station wagon's back section ("His leg hair touched my side of the seat!"), TV shows, whose room Toby the cat would sleep in, and even food in the refrigerator. Dan and I definitely duked it out enough to rub a few rough edges off each other, which is the whole point of sibling rivalry, experts say.

Now of course we get along fine and IM (instant message) each other about hockey scores and what our kids are up to. But naturally we're all grown up, and adults don't fight, do they?

Usually not, but grown-ups do their own version of the sibling smackdown. It's subtler, more genteel than a yelling, hair-pulling brawl. Instead, when we have a bone to pick with a friend, we seethe, resent, gossip, and make snide little jabs here and there when we can. The results can be even more devastating, because though we may not fight like kids anymore, we also don't make up as fast as little ones either. Without the resilient spirits our children seem to have, we lack the ability to snap out of our anger and commence our friendship together like nothing happened. When hurt, we grown-ups often stew about it and then find a socially acceptable way to get our pal back for whatever she did or said that has our knickers in a twist.

"She didn't come to my Tupperware party even though I came to hers!"

"I can't believe she made that joke about my weight. Just because she can afford a gym membership and I can't . . ."

"I worked incredibly hard on this teen moms project for church. It's totally unfair she was asked to head up the committee and I wasn't!"

Whatever the insult—or perception of insult, as is sometimes the case—we need to learn to let it go. As moms, we need our friends more than ever to support us and encourage us on our mothering journey and as women! We teach our kids to be kind and forgiving to their siblings, and we need to practice what we preach. The next time someone slaps you in the face—figuratively, let's hope!—take your hurt feeling to the God who loves you and forgives you all day every day. Ask him for the grace to let go of your grievance and the mercy to forgive.

Make sure that nobody pays back wrong for wrong,
but always try to be kind to each other and to everyone else.
1 Thessalonians 5:15

55: go to your room for "rest time"

May the words of my mouth and
the meditation of my heart be pleasing in
your sight, O LORD, my Rock and my Redeemer.

Psalm 19:14

If your kids are anything like mine, they *looove* going to their rooms for naptime, or if they've graduated to postnapping, "rest time." Yeah right. They love it about as much as gagging down lima beans and flossing. Mine usually trudge upstairs in a solemn fashion that suggests walking to a torture chamber.

Why do such cherubic children as mine and yours balk at the notion of rest time? I think somehow their little psyches must pick up on the fact that this allegedly beneficial time alone in their rooms reading or playing quietly may do Mom more good than it does them. (I can just see the wheels turning in their angelic little heads: *if this is good for Mommy, then what in the world does that have to do with me?*)

Like my kids, though, I sometimes resist slowing down for any significant period of time, never mind in silence. It's one thing to collapse on the couch, watching *Trading Spaces* and escaping the din of kids for an hour, and quite another to intentionally carve out time for quiet, reflection, listening, and prayer. We are used to hubbub and craziness and constant sounds. At the very least, the radio or TV is always on, like the soundtrack to our lives. Complete silence—though golden—is also a bit unnerving, isn't it? Modern moms need to cultivate the practice of quietness and meditation.

Psalm 119:99 says, "I have more insight than all my teachers, for I meditate on your statutes." Though David was from a culture that valued and cultivated meditation, we need to ditch some of our cultural baggage—busyness, action, do, do, do!—and learn to soak in the wisdom and truth of Scripture. As David learned, the practice of focusing attention on God and finding calmness in his company is invaluable. Meditation leads to wisdom, peace, strength, and joy.

I know it's incredibly tempting during a rare interlude of quiet to pick up toys or check your email or watch *Oprah*, but be sure you make time in your life to practice meditation. Choose one Bible verse or one aspect of God—his love, power, faithfulness, or some other character trait—and quietly contemplate it. The reason we make our kids have rest time is to force them to slow down, get comfortable in their own company, and rest their bodies and minds. (And let's not forget that it gives us a chance to think in complete sentences and possibly listen to a CD without the song "Someone's in the Kitchen with Dinah" on it.) Whether you meditate at night before bed, in the early morning, or during naptime, try to exercise your own "rest times" too. They'll stand you in good stead for the other 23.5 hours in your hectic day.

The unfolding of your words gives light;
it gives understanding to the simple.
Psalm 119:130

56: watch where you're stepping

Just as each of us has one body with
many members, and these members do not
all have the same function, so in Christ we
who are many form one body.

Romans 12:4–5

It was like a scene out of Currier and Ives, except for the buggies and the people in Victorian clothing. Our family was having one of those really warm and fuzzy Christmas evenings, complete with hot cocoa, Yuletide tunes, and hyper kids bouncing around the room. The box of ornaments had recently been hauled from the basement with grunts and groans, and it was time to trim the tree.

Being the Queen of Sap, I lovingly unfolded each ornament and reminisced about its provenance. The kids, of course, just wanted the tree to be up and running. My husband, with his low-sap threshold, began hanging ornaments a bit quicker than I would have liked. Actually, it was kind of getting on my nerves, the way he was speed-decorating the Christmas tree instead of fondling each ornament lovingly and giving a thirty-minute speech about what it meant to him.

Anyway, in his haste, Doyle looped this ceramic fish ornament on a branch that wasn't sturdy enough to hold it. The fish shattered on the wood floor, and the kids were commanded to jump up on the couch where their tender tootsies couldn't come in contact with shards of ceramic. We swept up all the pieces visible to the naked eye, except of course the one chunk camouflaged in the throw rug. About half an hour later, my second toe found that one.

I'll spare you the drama that ensued, but I will say the neighbors must have thought someone was being murdered next door. I'm not exactly the stoic type.

Days later when my poor little digit was still throbbing and I was hobbling around like a granny, it hit me: just one tiny toe was injured, yet my entire body was thrown off kilter. Because I was walking oddly, my other foot was doing all the work of hauling me around. Then my back started to ache because I was walking lopsided, and pretty soon I was in bad shape altogether. I couldn't even *shop* properly for Christmas—can you believe it?

The parallel was crystal clear. Romans 12 talks about the church being like a body with many body parts serving their own functions. I was struck by how one cut toe could so dramatically affect my back, my neck, my legs—my whole body! What happens when I, as a member of the body of Christ, don't fulfill my function by using my gifts? What if sin in my life cripples the usefulness God designed me for? No matter how small or insignificant the member is, I learned, if that part is injured or made useless in some way, it has wide-reaching ramifications for the entire body.

But in fact God has arranged the parts in the body, every one of them, just as he wanted them to be.

1 Corinthians 12:18

57: if you stick out that lip any farther . . .

And do not grumble, as some of them did.

1 Corinthians 10:10

My little guy, Ezra, has a world-class pouty lip. When an injury of some sort is perceived, he also likes to wrap his arms around himself, huff, puff, and generally take on airs of one sorely mistreated. The cause for such drama? The pizza may be "folded" wrong, or perhaps the plate is yellow and not green, his favorite color of the moment—you know, big stuff like that. Sometimes he even goes so far as to name his emotion: "Mommy, I feel werry grumb-el-ly."

Well, at least he knows he's grumbling. But like so many of God's children, a three-year-old with a jutted-out lip is wasting time and energy by griping, not to mention missing out on the blessings of a grateful heart. The Bible is rife with examples of people who complained (the Israelites and their famous "No manna, thank you" riffs), moaned (Remember Jonah and the worm?), and generally whined about their lives until God stepped in and did business with them.

One benefit of motherhood is that there are so many spiritual applications in our day-to-day lives with munchkins—if we are looking for them. As the mother of two lovely and adorable sons, who sometimes resort to whining in hopes of getting something they want, I have a much richer sense of how God must feel when his beloved children fuss at him. Whining makes me crazy, I must confess, so I also look at God's boundless patience with new awe. How is it possible that almighty God not only puts up with our grumbling hearts but forgives us time and time again and gently sets us on a path to gratitude?

Just as a tot's grumbling can be a cue to underlying causes—no nap, Mommy being on the phone *forever* (ten minutes), or something else—our complaints are usually symptomatic of a disconnect with our Father. The remedy is to look up from our disgruntlement and check out all the things we have to be grateful for. Like us moms, God loves it when we come to him with a spirit of thanksgiving. Paul seldom mentioned prayer in the New Testament without conveying an attitude of gratitude. "Be joyful always; pray continually; give thanks in all circumstances," he writes in 1 Thessalonians 5:16–18.

Wouldn't it be great if our little tykes came to us with happy, contented hearts, glad to see us and be with us, and thankful for the care and feeding we give? It happens sometimes, and when it does, we would give them the moon if they asked. Next time your child whines ("But I don't wanna go to Great-aunt Ethel's for lunch!"), use it as a flashpoint to assess your own grumbles-to-gratitude ratio. Then ask the Giver of all good things to help you be more thankful about who he is and what he does. Ask him to cultivate in you a spirit of gratitude and contentment and to show you how to teach your children to be thankful too.

Let us come before him with thanksgiving
and extol him with music and song.

Psalm 95:2

58: eat your vegetables

Our fathers [and mothers] disciplined us
for a little while as they thought best
but God disciplines us for our good,
that we may share in his holiness.

Hebrews 12:10

What is it about kids and vegetables? The only child I've ever known to profess a love for green food (and gummy worms don't count), is Vivienne, a baba ghanoush, lentil stew, pureed leek–eating child of my acquaintance. I remember going out for Indian food with Vivi's family when my son Jonah was a toddler. He gaped at his little friend with utter amazement as she shoveled in spoonfuls of Palak Paneer, a cheese and spinach puree, while he himself was struggling with a piece of flatbread and a few particles of curried rice. There wasn't any way Jonah was going to ingest the green stuff unless he was being tube fed with it.

Of course, as his mother and on-site dietician, it behooves me to push veggies upon my child every chance I get. Why insist that a little boy sit at the dinner table until his broccoli (slathered with cheese, usually) is all eaten? Because broccoli has Vitamin

C and A and fiber and all that good stuff necessary for optimum health, that's why! As moms we do what we think is best for our kids. Brussels sprouts may not be pretty—or tasty—but we serve them anyway because they are for our kids' own good.

Sometimes our Father insists on giving us doses of hard-to-swallow situations and people in our lives because doing so is for our benefit. The little girl from down the street who pounds on the door "coincidentally" just as you're sitting down with your family to eat pizza. The difficulty of trusting that God will provide finances to fix the lemon-van (er, minivan). A grouchy co-worker who makes your job so much harder. We may screw up our faces in dismay as we consider some of the unpalatable elements that make us feel put upon and hassled. But God is using the "yucky stuff" to build compassion, trust, longsuffering, and other positive character traits into our lives. He loves us too much to let us skate through a candy-coated life.

So next time you're sneaking some zucchini into the Spaghetti-O's, remember why you're doing it, and especially why God does the same thing to you—and *for* you.

Shall we accept good from God, and not trouble?

Job 2:10

59: there's no such thing as the boogeyman

Who of you by worrying can
add a single hour to [her] life?

Luke 12:25

Last night I explained for the seventy-fifth time that the only monsters out there are nice, friendly ones like Elmo, Grover, and Sully. "I skeered of *mon*-ters, Mommy," my two-year-old, Ezra, said, eyes wide with dread. I comforted him as best I could, cuddling a little extra, throwing his closet doors open, and flipping a bright night-light on so he could see for himself that no hideous, scaly monstrosities were hiding inside. I prayed with him that Jesus would be with him and keep him safe. Thankfully, this round of "I skeered, Mommy," didn't require any heavy-duty solutions like spritzing "monster spray" under the bed, in the closet, in the drawers, and so on. (You gotta dust sometime, right?) This time my little one took me at my word.

I'm quite sure my Father wishes I would also take him at his word and believe that he will protect and care for me and my family. I admit I often fret about the "boogeyman"—whoever he is—and what harm might possibly come to my precious boys. You know what it's like to look at your child (it helps when they are sleeping angelically), your heart swelling with love and that ferocious mother bear protectiveness, when suddenly you imagine any and all terrible things that could happen.

I remember when Jonah was a tiny baby and we lived in an iffy, borderline neighborhood between the "hood" and some beautiful homes. Some strange notions would pop into my head, like maybe some crackhead would kidnap my perfect baby for the black market. It wasn't very likely at all, but still I indulged my paranoid imaginings! Then there's my pal Bonnie, a sensible, unflappable woman who usually doesn't suffer from nervous delusions. But when her first baby came along, and the wee angel had a scratch on her hand around the same time that a Canadian political leader had that flesh-eating bacteria thing—well! The power of suggestion is mighty strong, and pretty soon Bonnie was wondering if Suzanne might have the same thing. That's a new mom for you!

Worrying, stressing, Technicolor imagining—these activities do as much good as misting monster spray all over yourself. The Bible is clear that worry accomplishes nothing, not to mention that it is counterproductive. Worry can blot out peace, joy, and spiritual growth in our lives. Wallowing in it can produce stress hormones that can even make us sick. So how do we whack away at worry? Start by handing over your anxious thoughts to the one who knows all, sees all, and controls all. Your Father wants to lift the burden of worry from your heart and carry it. He wants you to grow in obedience and trust as you learn to hand all the little and big fears you have to him. Journal your worrisome thoughts to give them perspective and clarity. Tell Satan to get behind you, because he wants you to be filled with fear. And pray for your children's well-being. It's the only surefire way to diminish the power of worry and replace it with peace.

The peace of God, which transcends all understanding,
will guard your hearts and your minds in Christ Jesus.

Philippians 4:7

60: the kitchen is closed

Better one handful with tranquility
than two handfuls with toil.

Ecclesiastes 4:6

"Mom-meeee, I wanna snack!" My son yells this rather obnoxious plea from across the house, unmindful of the fact that he is breaking multiple rules—such as saying "please" and not bellowing—in one fell swoop. After a long, muggy summer day, juggling three meals and intermittent requests for cold drinks and ice-cream treats ("Sam has the SpongeBob SquarePants kind, Mom"), this mom is ready for a break.

Do you ever feel like everyone wants a piece of you? The family needs to eat well-balanced, appealing meals, which is no small feat when your idea of domesticity is ordering pizza on the speed dial. And that's just the bipeds in the home. The dog needs vittles, the kitten needs chow, and even Judy the snail (don't ask) could use a fresh lettuce leaf to nibble on. It's enough to cause even the most devoted, nurturing mother to collapse in a heap, stymied by the incessant demands of motherhood. I don't know about you, but sometimes I feel that if one more being (human, canine, mollusk—whatever) asks for food from the mother hand, I'm going to blow.

Yup, the kitchen is most definitely closed, and that's a good thing. It's time for mom to go to the bookstore/café and sip a mocha latte, pop in a chick flick on the DVD player, or just do her nails. We all need breathers big and small built into our lives so we can continue to serve our families with grace and cheer. God created us with the need—that's *need,* not simply want—to have balance and respite from our many duties. You're not a bad mom if you take time to re-create yourself when you have unwrapped one too many Popsicles. In fact, you're really doing your family a big favor when you dole out a little TLC for yourself. Mary Byers, author of *The Mother Load,* extols the benefits of "closing the kitchen," even for a few minutes: "I try to practice the art of simply existing for at least five minutes a day. It's difficult. But spending time doing nothing often produces great results: ideas flow, thanksgiving wells up in my soul. Peace settles in, energy is restored. And more than anything, I reconnect with a sense of deep purpose."[8]

Carve out time for spiritual and personal renewal. Go to the library—by yourself—on the way home from grocery shopping once a week. Call a friend and go see the new Gwyneth Paltrow movie—something your husband may not want to see. (Put dates with friends on the calendar, which is the only way to make them stick.) Walk a few nights a week with a neighbor friend. Check out which concerts are coming to town and splurge on a couple of tickets for you and your man. Get a Pilates video and work out the kinks when your kids are in bed. My point is, actively seek out ways to rejuvenate that woman inside you who may be buried under "the mother load," so to speak.

Every woman has different levels of responsibility and stress she can handle, so remember that next time Becky Home-Ec-y down the street is whipping up a sorbet or soufflé or whatever. The question is, what do *you* need in order to keep your life in equilibrium and wellness? Pray about it and ask your Father to help you live your best, most balanced life. You'll have energy to exercise your spiritual gifts and to be a better friend, wife, mother, daughter, and employee. Open your hands to tranquility, as Solomon put it, and the toil will take care of itself (for an hour or two anyway!).

Come to me, all you who are weary and burdened,
and I will give you rest.

Matthew 11:28

notes

1. Bruce Wilkinson, *Secrets of the Vine* (Sisters, OR: Multnomah, 2001).

2. Lisa Tawn Bergren, *God Encounter: Experiencing the Power of Creative Prayer* (Colorado Springs: Waterbrook, 2002), 84.

3. Ibid.

4. Lorilee Craker, *See How They Run: An Energizing Guide to Keeping Up with Your Turbo-Toddler* (Colorado Springs: Waterbrook, 2004), 20.

5. Lisa Whelchel, *The Facts of Life: And Other Lessons My Father Taught Me* (Sisters, OR: Multnomah, 2001), 156–57.

6. Louise Bergmann DuMont, *Grace by the Cup: A Break from the Daily Grind* (Grand Rapids: Revell, 2003), 40.

7. Silvana Clark, *Stuffed Animals on the Ceiling Fan* (Grand Rapids: Revell, 2003), 145.

8. Mary Byers, *The Mother Load* (Eugene, OR: Harvest House, 2005).

Lorilee Craker lives in Grand Rapids, Michigan, where she is an entertainment writer for the *Grand Rapids Press*. Drawing on her life with her husband, Doyle, and three children, Lorilee is the author of several books for young moms, including *When the Belly Button Pops, the Baby's Done* and *We Should Do This More Often: A Parent's Guide to Romance, Passion, and Other Prechild Activities You Vaguely Recall*. Contact her via her website, www.LorileeCraker.com.

About MOPS

You take care of your children, Mom. Who takes care of you? MOPS International (Mothers of Preschoolers) provides mothers of preschoolers with the nurture and resources they need to be the best moms they can be.

MOPS is dedicated to the message that "mothering matters," and that moms of young children need encouragement during these critical and formative years. Chartered groups meet in more than 3,600 churches and Christian ministries throughout the United States and in 30 other countries. Each MOPS program helps mothers find friendship and acceptance, provides opportunities for women to develop and practice leadership skills in the group, and promotes spiritual growth. MOPS groups are chartered ministries of local churches and meet at a variety of times and locations: daytime, evenings, and on weekends; in churches, homes, and workplaces.

The MOPPETS program offers a loving, learning experience for children while their moms attend MOPS. Other MOPS resources include *MOMSense* magazine and radio, the MOPS International website, and books and resources available through the MOPShop.

With 14.3 million mothers of preschoolers in the United States alone, many moms can't attend a local MOPS group. These moms still need the support that MOPS International can offer! For a small registration fee, any mother of preschoolers can join the MOPS♥to♥Mom Connection and receive *MOMSense* magazine six times a year, a weekly Mom-E-Mail message of encouragement, and other valuable benefits.

Find out how MOPS International can help you become part of the MOPS♥to♥Mom Connection and/or join or start a MOPS group. Visit our website at www.MOPS.org. Phone us at 303-733-5353. Or email Info@MOPS.org. To learn how to start a MOPS group, call 1-888-910-MOPS.